Butter Bean Bl[...] Healthy Ways to Savor this Versatile Legume

Myla Affordable Emery

Copyright © 2024 Myla Affordable Emery
All rights reserved.
:

Contents

INTRODUCTION 8

1. Classic Butter Bean Hummus 10
2. Garlic and Herb Butter Bean Spread 11
3. Roasted Red Pepper Butter Bean Dip 12
4. Lemon Rosemary Butter Bean Dip 14
5. Spicy Sriracha Butter Bean Dip 15
6. Butter Bean and Avocado Dip 16
7. Butter Bean and Artichoke Dip 17
8. Mediterranean Butter Bean Dip 19
9. Creamy Butter Bean and Basil Pesto Dip 20
10. Smoky Chipotle Butter Bean Dip 21
11. Butter Bean and Sun-Dried Tomato Tapenade 22
12. Butter Bean and Feta Cheese Dip 24
13. Creamy Butter Bean and Roasted Garlic Dip 25
14. Thai-Inspired Butter Bean Dip 27
15. Butter Bean and Spinach Dip 28
16. Butter Bean and Cilantro Hummus 29
17. Roasted Eggplant and Butter Bean Dip 31
18. Sweet Potato and Butter Bean Hummus 32
19. Butter Bean and Walnut Dip 33
20. Spiced Pumpkin Butter Bean Dip 35
21. Curried Butter Bean Dip 36
22. Black Olive and Butter Bean Tapenade 38
23. Butter Bean and Roasted Red Onion Dip 39
24. Butter Bean and Roasted Beet Hummus 41
25. Butter Bean and Caramelized Onion Dip 42
26. Creamy Butter Bean and Dill Dip 43
27. Butter Bean and Smoked Paprika Dip 44

28. Roasted Carrot and Butter Bean Hummus 46
29. Butter Bean and Sunflower Seed Dip 47
30. Butter Bean and Minted Pea Dip..49
31. Roasted Tomato and Butter Bean Dip 50
32. Butter Bean and Charred Corn Hummus................................51
33. Butter Bean and Herbed Ricotta Dip......................................53
34. Butter Bean and Green Chile Dip 54
35. Butter Bean and Lemon Zest Hummus 56
36. Butter Bean and Horseradish Dip 57
37. Butter Bean and Cranberry Dip 58
38. Roasted Red Cabbage and Butter Bean Hummus 60
39. Butter Bean and Goat Cheese Dip 61
40. Butter Bean and Caper Tapenade 62
41. Butter Bean and Miso Dip 64
42. Butter Bean and Tzatziki Hummus 65
43. Butter Bean and Honey Mustard Dip 66
44. Creamy Butter Bean and Sage Dip 68
45. Roasted Red Kale and Butter Bean Hummus 69
46. Butter Bean and Pomegranate Dip...70
47. Butter Bean and Gorgonzola Dip...72
48. Butter Bean and Green Onion Hummus 73
49. Butter Bean and Cucumber Dip 75
50. Butter Bean and Roasted Eggplant Hummus..........................76
51. Butter Bean and Lemon Pepper Dip 78
52. Roasted Garlic and Butter Bean Hummus..............................79
53. Butter Bean and Za'atar Dip...81
54. Butter Bean and Harissa Hummus 82
55. Butter Bean and Mango Salsa..83
56. Butter Bean and Roasted Tomato Salsa.................................84

57. Butter Bean and Pine Nut Dip 86

58. Butter Bean and Roasted Carrot Hummus 87

59. Butter Bean and Kimchi Dip 88

60. Butter Bean and Jalapeño Hummus 90

61. Butter Bean and Cumin Dip 91

62. Butter Bean and Tomato Basil Dip 93

63. Butter Bean and Pickled Radish Salsa 94

64. Butter Bean and Avocado Hummus 95

65. Butter Bean and Roasted Red Pepper Salsa 96

66. Butter Bean and Cilantro Pesto 98

67. Butter Bean and Green Olive Tapenade 99

68. Butter Bean and Smoked Almond Dip 100

69. Butter Bean and Cinnamon Hummus 102

70. Butter Bean and Pickled Jalapeño Dip 103

71. Butter Bean and Cashew Spread 104

72. Butter Bean and Roasted Garlic Pesto 106

73. Butter Bean and Chili-Lime Salsa 107

74. Butter Bean and Paprika Dip 109

75. Butter Bean and Mango Chutney 110

76. Butter Bean and Roasted Bell Pepper Hummus 111

77. Butter Bean and Black Bean Salsa 113

78. Butter Bean and Ginger Dip 114

79. Butter Bean and Roasted Butternut Squash Hummus 115

80. Butter Bean and Saffron Aioli 116

81. Butter Bean and Black Olive Hummus 118

82. Butter Bean and Cranberry Salsa 119

83. Butter Bean and Walnut Pesto 120

84. Butter Bean and Pomegranate Salsa 122

85. Butter Bean and Roasted Jalapeño Hummus 123

86. Butter Bean and Curry Dip 125

87. Butter Bean and Salsa Verde 126

88. Butter Bean and Pineapple Salsa 127

89. Butter Bean and Hazelnut Pesto 129

90. Butter Bean and Mango Salsa Verde 130

91. Butter Bean and Pickled Ginger Dip 131

92. Butter Bean and Chili Mango Salsa 132

93. Butter Bean and Roasted Red Chili Hummus 134

94. Butter Bean and Smoky Paprika Pesto 135

95. Butter Bean and Roasted Green Chile Salsa 136

96. Butter Bean and Cilantro Chimichurri 138

97. Butter Bean and Cranberry Chutney 139

98. Butter Bean and Walnut-Basil Pesto 140

99. Butter Bean and Charred Lemon Hummus 142

100. Butter Bean and Za'atar Pesto 143

CONCLUSION 145

INTRODUCTION

Welcome to *Butter Bean Bliss: 100 Healthy Ways to Savor this Versatile Legume*. In these pages, we embark on a culinary journey celebrating the butter bean—also known as lima bean—a humble yet immensely versatile legume cherished in kitchens around the world. Whether you're a seasoned chef or a novice cook, this cookbook offers a myriad of delightful recipes that showcase the butter bean's unique flavor and nutritional benefits.

Discovering the Butter Bean

The butter bean, with its creamy texture and mild, buttery taste, has been a staple in kitchens for centuries. Originating in South America and later cultivated across continents, it has found its way into diverse cuisines, adapting to local flavors and culinary traditions. From hearty stews in the Mediterranean to succulent salads in the American South, the butter bean's adaptability makes it a star ingredient in dishes both simple and sophisticated.

Nutritional Powerhouse

Beyond its culinary appeal, the butter bean packs a nutritious punch. High in protein, fiber, and essential vitamins and minerals, including folate, magnesium, and iron, it is a wholesome addition to any diet. Its low glycemic index also makes it a favorable choice for those managing blood sugar levels. Whether you're looking to boost your protein intake or simply incorporate more nutrient-dense foods into your meals, butter beans offer a delicious and healthful option.

From Pantry to Plate

In *Butter Bean Bliss*, you'll find a treasure trove of recipes that highlight the butter bean's versatility. From comforting soups and stews to vibrant salads and savory mains, each recipe has been carefully crafted to bring out the best of this delightful legume. Whether you prefer classic combinations or daring new flavors, there's something here to tantalize every palate.

Cooking with Confidence

Cooking with butter beans doesn't require culinary expertise—all you need is a willingness to experiment and a desire to explore new flavors. Throughout this cookbook, you'll find tips on selecting, storing, and preparing butter beans, ensuring that every dish you create is a testament to their natural goodness.

Embracing a Healthy Lifestyle

At its heart, *Butter Bean Bliss* is more than just a collection of recipes—it's a guide to embracing a healthy lifestyle through mindful eating. By incorporating butter beans into your meals, you're not only treating yourself to delicious flavors but also nourishing your body with wholesome, nutritious food.

Join us on this culinary adventure as we celebrate the butter bean in all its glory. Whether you're seeking inspiration for a weeknight dinner or planning a special gathering, let *Butter Bean Bliss* be your companion in discovering the joy of cooking with this versatile and nutritious legume.

1. Classic Butter Bean Hummus

Elevate your culinary experience with this delightful recipe for Classic Butter Bean Hummus. Bursting with wholesome flavors and rich in protein, this twist on traditional hummus introduces butter beans as the star ingredient. The creamy texture and nutty undertones of butter beans blend seamlessly with the familiar hummus profile, creating a nutritious and satisfying dip or spread. Perfect for those seeking a healthy alternative, this recipe is a testament to the versatility of butter beans in the kitchen.

Serving: Makes approximately 2 cups of Classic Butter Bean Hummus.
Preparation Time: 15 minutes
Ready Time: 15 minutes

Ingredients:
- 2 cups cooked butter beans (canned or boiled)
- 1/4 cup tahini
- 2 cloves garlic, minced
- 1/4 cup extra-virgin olive oil
- Juice of 1 lemon
- 1 teaspoon ground cumin
- 1/2 teaspoon paprika
- Salt and pepper to taste
- 2-3 tablespoons water (adjust for desired consistency)
- Optional toppings: drizzle of olive oil, sprinkle of paprika, chopped fresh parsley

Instructions:
1. Prepare Butter Beans: If using canned butter beans, drain and rinse them under cold water. If using dried beans, cook them according to package instructions until tender.
2. Combine Ingredients: In a food processor, combine the cooked butter beans, tahini, minced garlic, olive oil, lemon juice, ground cumin, paprika, salt, and pepper.
3. Blend: Process the ingredients until smooth, scraping down the sides of the bowl as needed. If the mixture is too thick, add water, one tablespoon at a time, until you achieve your desired consistency.

4. Taste and Adjust: Taste the hummus and adjust the seasoning if necessary. You can add more salt, pepper, or lemon juice to suit your preferences.
5. Serve: Transfer the Classic Butter Bean Hummus to a serving bowl. Drizzle with olive oil, sprinkle with paprika, and garnish with chopped fresh parsley for a burst of color.
6. Enjoy: Serve the hummus with your favorite veggies, pita bread, or as a spread on sandwiches. Enjoy this nutritious and flavorful twist on traditional hummus!

Nutrition Information:
Note: Nutrition Information is approximate and may vary based on specific ingredients used.
- Calories per serving: 150, Total Fat: 10g, Saturated Fat: 1.5g, Trans Fat: 0g, Cholesterol: 0mg, Sodium: 180mg, Total Carbohydrates: 12g, Dietary Fiber: 3g, Sugars: 0g, Protein: 5g

This Classic Butter Bean Hummus is a delicious and health-conscious addition to your culinary repertoire, showcasing the versatility and nutritional benefits of butter beans.

2. Garlic and Herb Butter Bean Spread

Elevate your culinary experience with this nutritious and flavorful Garlic and Herb Butter Bean Spread. Packed with protein, fiber, and a medley of aromatic herbs, this spread is not only a delicious addition to your meals but also a fantastic way to incorporate the health benefits of butter beans into your diet. Versatile and easy to make, it's a must-try for anyone seeking a wholesome and satisfying spread that's perfect for various occasions.

Serving: Makes approximately 1 ½ cups of Garlic and Herb Butter Bean Spread.
Preparation Time: 15 minutes
Ready Time: 15 minutes

Ingredients:
- 2 cans (15 ounces each) butter beans, drained and rinsed
- 3 cloves garlic, minced

- 2 tablespoons fresh parsley, finely chopped
- 1 tablespoon fresh thyme leaves, stripped from stems
- 1 teaspoon fresh rosemary, finely chopped
- 1/4 cup extra-virgin olive oil
- 2 tablespoons lemon juice
- Salt and black pepper to taste

Instructions:
1. In a food processor, combine the butter beans, minced garlic, parsley, thyme, and rosemary.
2. Pulse the mixture until it starts to break down.
3. With the food processor running, slowly pour in the olive oil and lemon juice. Continue processing until the spread reaches a smooth and creamy consistency.
4. Stop and scrape down the sides of the food processor as needed. Taste the spread and add salt and black pepper to your liking. Blend again to incorporate the seasonings.
5. Transfer the Garlic and Herb Butter Bean Spread to a bowl and refrigerate for at least 30 minutes to allow the flavors to meld.
6. Serve the spread on whole-grain crackers, as a dip for fresh vegetables, or as a savory sandwich spread.

Nutrition Information:
(Per 2-tablespoon serving)
- Calories: 90, Total Fat: 5g, Saturated Fat: 0.5g, Trans Fat: 0g, Cholesterol: 0mg, Sodium: 120mg, Total Carbohydrates: 8g, Dietary Fiber: 2g, Sugars: 0g, Protein: 3g

This Garlic and Herb Butter Bean Spread not only delights the taste buds but also contributes to a healthy and balanced diet. Enjoy the rich flavors and nutritional benefits in every bite!

3. Roasted Red Pepper Butter Bean Dip

Elevate your snack game with this nutritious and flavorful Roasted Red Pepper Butter Bean Dip. Butter beans, also known as lima beans, take center stage in this wholesome dip, providing a creamy base that's high in protein and fiber. Paired with the smoky sweetness of roasted red peppers, this dip is a delightful combination of taste and health. Perfect for parties or a quick and satisfying snack, this recipe is a must-try for those looking to add a nutritious twist to their appetizer spread.

Serving: Makes approximately 2 cups of dip.
Preparation Time: 15 minutes
Ready Time: 30 minutes

Ingredients:
- 1 can (15 ounces) butter beans, drained and rinsed
- 1 cup roasted red peppers, drained if from a jar
- 2 cloves garlic, minced
- 2 tablespoons tahini
- 2 tablespoons extra-virgin olive oil
- 1 tablespoon lemon juice
- 1 teaspoon ground cumin
- 1/2 teaspoon smoked paprika
- Salt and pepper to taste
- Fresh parsley for garnish (optional)

Instructions:
1. In a food processor, combine the butter beans, roasted red peppers, minced garlic, tahini, olive oil, lemon juice, ground cumin, and smoked paprika.
2. Process the ingredients until smooth and creamy, scraping down the sides of the bowl as needed. If the dip is too thick, you can add a bit more olive oil or water to reach your desired consistency.
3. Taste the dip and season with salt and pepper to your liking. Blend again to incorporate the seasonings.
4. Once the dip reaches a smooth consistency and balanced flavor, transfer it to a serving bowl.
5. If desired, garnish the dip with fresh parsley for a burst of color and added freshness.
6. Serve the Roasted Red Pepper Butter Bean Dip with your favorite vegetable sticks, whole-grain crackers, or pita bread.

Nutrition Information:
(Note: Nutrition Information may vary based on specific brands and quantities used.)
- Serving Size: 2 tablespoons

- Calories: 60, Total Fat: 4g, Saturated Fat: 0.5g, Cholesterol: 0mg, Sodium: 80mg, Total Carbohydrates: 5g, Dietary Fiber: 1g, Sugars: 0g, Protein: 2g

Enjoy this Roasted Red Pepper Butter Bean Dip as a tasty and health-conscious addition to your repertoire of butter bean recipes.

4. Lemon Rosemary Butter Bean Dip

Indulge in the vibrant flavors of this nutritious and zesty Lemon Rosemary Butter Bean Dip. Packed with protein-rich butter beans, fresh lemon, and aromatic rosemary, this dip is not only delicious but also a wholesome addition to your snack repertoire. Perfect for gatherings or as a healthy spread, this recipe celebrates the versatility of butter beans in a delightful and flavorful way.

Serving: Makes approximately 2 cups of dip
Preparation Time: 15 minutes
Ready Time: 15 minutes

Ingredients:
- 2 cans (15 ounces each) butter beans, drained and rinsed
- 1/4 cup extra-virgin olive oil
- 2 tablespoons fresh lemon juice
- 1 teaspoon lemon zest
- 2 cloves garlic, minced
- 1 teaspoon fresh rosemary, finely chopped
- Salt and pepper to taste
- Optional: Red pepper flakes for a hint of heat

Instructions:
1. In a food processor, combine the butter beans, olive oil, lemon juice, lemon zest, minced garlic, and chopped rosemary.
2. Blend the ingredients until smooth, scraping down the sides of the food processor as needed.
3. Season the dip with salt and pepper to taste. For a touch of heat, add red pepper flakes if desired.
4. Continue blending until the dip reaches a creamy consistency, adjusting seasoning as needed.

5. Transfer the Lemon Rosemary Butter Bean Dip to a serving bowl.

Nutrition Information:
Note: Nutrition Information may vary based on specific brands and quantities used.
- Serving Size: 2 tablespoons
- Calories: 60, Total Fat: 4g, Saturated Fat: 0.5g, Cholesterol: 0mg, Sodium: 80mg, Total Carbohydrates: 5g, Dietary Fiber: 1g, Sugars: 0g, Protein: 2g

Tip:
Pair this Lemon Rosemary Butter Bean Dip with crisp, fresh vegetables or whole-grain crackers for a satisfying and health-conscious snack. Enjoy the goodness of butter beans in a flavorful and nutrient-packed dip that's perfect for any occasion.

5. Spicy Sriracha Butter Bean Dip

Elevate your snack game with this Spicy Sriracha Butter Bean Dip, a delightful twist on a classic bean dip. Butter beans, known for their creamy texture and mild flavor, take center stage in this recipe, complemented by the bold kick of Sriracha and the rich goodness of butter. This dip is not only a flavorful indulgence but also a healthy option for those seeking a protein-packed, fiber-rich snack. Perfect for gatherings or a solo treat, this Spicy Sriracha Butter Bean Dip is sure to become a favorite in your repertoire of healthy, delicious recipes.

Serving: 6-8
Preparation time: 15 minutes
Ready time: 25 minutes

Ingredients:
- 2 cans (15 oz each) butter beans, drained and rinsed
- 1/4 cup olive oil
- 3 cloves garlic, minced
- 2 tablespoons Sriracha sauce (adjust to taste)
- 1 tablespoon lemon juice
- 2 tablespoons unsalted butter
- 1 teaspoon ground cumin
- 1 teaspoon paprika

- Salt and pepper to taste
- Fresh cilantro or parsley for garnish (optional)

Instructions:
1. Preheat your oven to 375°F (190°C).
2. In a food processor, combine the butter beans, olive oil, minced garlic, Sriracha sauce, lemon juice, unsalted butter, ground cumin, and paprika. Season with salt and pepper to taste.
3. Blend the mixture until smooth and creamy, scraping down the sides as needed to ensure all ingredients are well incorporated.
4. Transfer the dip into an oven-safe dish and smooth the top with a spatula.
5. Bake in the preheated oven for 15-20 minutes or until the edges are golden brown and the dip is heated through.
6. Remove from the oven and let it cool for a few minutes before serving.
7. Garnish with fresh cilantro or parsley if desired.

Nutrition Information:
(Per serving - based on 8 servings)
- Calories: 180, Total Fat: 12g, Saturated Fat: 3.5g, Cholesterol: 10mg, Sodium: 260mg, Total Carbohydrates: 14g, Dietary Fiber: 4g, Sugars: 1g, Protein: 5g

Dip into this Spicy Sriracha Butter Bean Dip with your favorite veggies or whole-grain crackers for a wholesome and satisfying snack that brings together the goodness of butter beans and the bold flavors of Sriracha.

6. Butter Bean and Avocado Dip

Elevate your healthy eating with this delightful Butter Bean and Avocado Dip—a nutritious and flavorful option that combines the creamy goodness of butter beans with the rich texture of ripe avocados. Packed with protein, fiber, and essential nutrients, this dip is a versatile addition to your culinary repertoire. Whether served as a party appetizer or a wholesome snack, this recipe proves that healthy eating can be both delicious and satisfying.

Serving: Makes approximately 2 cups of dip.

Preparation Time: 15 minutes
Ready Time: 15 minutes

Ingredients:
- 1 can (15 ounces) butter beans, drained and rinsed
- 1 ripe avocado, peeled and pitted
- 2 tablespoons fresh lemon juice
- 2 cloves garlic, minced
- 2 tablespoons olive oil
- 1 teaspoon ground cumin
- Salt and pepper to taste
- Optional toppings: chopped fresh cilantro, cherry tomatoes, or a drizzle of olive oil

Instructions:
1. In a food processor, combine the butter beans, avocado, lemon juice, minced garlic, olive oil, and ground cumin.
2. Blend the ingredients until smooth and creamy, scraping down the sides of the processor as needed.
3. Season the dip with salt and pepper to taste. Adjust the seasoning according to your preferences.
4. Transfer the dip to a serving bowl and garnish with optional toppings such as chopped fresh cilantro, cherry tomatoes, or a drizzle of olive oil.
5. Serve the Butter Bean and Avocado Dip with your favorite whole-grain crackers, vegetable sticks, or pita bread.

Nutrition Information:
(Per 2-tablespoon serving)
- Calories: 80, Total Fat: 6g, Saturated Fat: 1g, Trans Fat: 0g, Cholesterol: 0mg, Sodium: 80mg, Total Carbohydrates: 6g, Dietary Fiber: 3g, Sugars: 0g, Protein: 2g

Note: Nutrition Information is approximate and may vary based on specific ingredients and serving sizes.

7. Butter Bean and Artichoke Dip

Elevate your snacking experience with this wholesome and flavorful Butter Bean and Artichoke Dip. Packed with protein, fiber, and nutrients, this dip not only satisfies your taste buds but also contributes to your well-being. Butter beans, known for their creamy texture, blend seamlessly with the richness of artichokes, creating a dip that's as nutritious as it is delicious. Serve it as an appetizer at gatherings or enjoy it as a guilt-free indulgence any time of day.

Serving: Makes approximately 2 cups of dip
Preparation Time: 15 minutes
Ready Time: 45 minutes

Ingredients:
- 1 can (15 ounces) butter beans, drained and rinsed
- 1 can (14 ounces) artichoke hearts, drained and chopped
- 1/4 cup extra-virgin olive oil
- 2 cloves garlic, minced
- 1 tablespoon lemon juice
- 1 teaspoon dried oregano
- 1/2 teaspoon ground cumin
- Salt and black pepper, to taste
- 1/4 cup chopped fresh parsley, for garnish (optional)

Instructions:
1. Preheat your oven to 375°F (190°C).
2. In a food processor, combine the butter beans, chopped artichoke hearts, olive oil, minced garlic, lemon juice, dried oregano, ground cumin, salt, and black pepper.
3. Blend the ingredients until the mixture becomes a smooth and creamy consistency.
4. Transfer the dip to an oven-safe dish, spreading it evenly.
5. Bake in the preheated oven for approximately 30 minutes, or until the edges are golden brown, and the dip is heated through.
6. Remove from the oven and let it cool for 10-15 minutes.
7. Garnish with chopped fresh parsley, if desired.
8. Serve the Butter Bean and Artichoke Dip with your favorite whole-grain crackers, vegetable sticks, or pita chips.

Nutrition Information:
(Per 2-tablespoon serving)

- Calories: 80, Total Fat: 5g, Saturated Fat: 0.7g, Trans Fat: 0g, Cholesterol: 0mg, Sodium: 180mg, Total Carbohydrates: 7g, Dietary Fiber: 2g, Sugars: 0.5g, Protein: 2.5g
Note: Nutrition Information may vary based on specific brands and quantities of ingredients used.

8. Mediterranean Butter Bean Dip

Dive into the heart of the Mediterranean with this delightful Butter Bean Dip. Packed with flavors inspired by the region's rich culinary tradition, this recipe transforms humble butter beans into a creamy and savory delight. Whether you're hosting a gathering or looking for a wholesome snack, this dip is a perfect choice. Embrace the health benefits of butter beans with this easy-to-make, nutritious, and delicious Mediterranean Butter Bean Dip.

Serving: Ideal for sharing, this recipe serves 6.
Preparation Time: 15 minutes
Ready Time: 20 minutes

Ingredients:
- 2 cans (15 ounces each) butter beans, drained and rinsed
- 1/4 cup extra-virgin olive oil
- 2 tablespoons tahini
- 2 cloves garlic, minced
- 1 teaspoon ground cumin
- Juice of 1 lemon
- Salt and pepper, to taste
- 2 tablespoons fresh parsley, chopped (for garnish)
- Optional: 1/2 teaspoon red pepper flakes for a hint of spice

Instructions:
1. In a food processor, combine the butter beans, olive oil, tahini, minced garlic, ground cumin, and lemon juice.
2. Process the mixture until smooth and creamy. If needed, scrape down the sides of the processor to ensure all ingredients are well incorporated.
3. Season the dip with salt and pepper to taste. Adjust the seasonings as per your preference.

4. If you prefer a bit of heat, add red pepper flakes and pulse to combine.
5. Transfer the dip to a serving bowl, drizzle with a bit of extra olive oil, and garnish with fresh chopped parsley.
6. Serve the Mediterranean Butter Bean Dip with an assortment of fresh vegetables, pita bread, or whole-grain crackers.

Nutrition Information:
(Per serving)
- Calories: 180, Total Fat: 10g, Saturated Fat: 1.5g, Trans Fat: 0g, Cholesterol: 0mg, Sodium: 250mg, Total Carbohydrates: 19g, Dietary Fiber: 6g, Sugars: 1g, Protein: 6g

Indulge in the robust flavors of the Mediterranean while embracing the nutritional benefits of butter beans with this Healthy Butter Bean Dip. Enjoy this wholesome dip as a tasty snack or a delightful appetizer at your next gathering!

9. Creamy Butter Bean and Basil Pesto Dip

Embrace the goodness of butter beans with this delightful and nutritious Creamy Butter Bean and Basil Pesto Dip. Butter beans, also known as lima beans, bring a rich and velvety texture to this dip, while the aromatic basil pesto adds a burst of freshness. This recipe is not only a flavorful appetizer but also a great way to incorporate the health benefits of butter beans into your diet. Perfect for parties or as a wholesome snack, this dip is sure to be a crowd-pleaser.

Serving: Ideal for 6-8 servings.
Preparation Time: 15 minutes
Ready Time: 15 minutes

Ingredients:
- 2 cans (15 ounces each) butter beans, drained and rinsed
- 1/3 cup extra-virgin olive oil
- 1/2 cup fresh basil leaves, packed
- 1/4 cup grated Parmesan cheese
- 2 cloves garlic, minced
- 2 tablespoons pine nuts, toasted
- 1 tablespoon lemon juice

- Salt and pepper to taste
- 2 tablespoons Greek yogurt (optional, for extra creaminess)
- Fresh vegetables and whole-grain crackers for serving

Instructions:
1. In a food processor, combine the butter beans, olive oil, basil, Parmesan cheese, garlic, pine nuts, and lemon juice.
2. Pulse the ingredients until smooth, scraping down the sides of the processor as needed.
3. If desired, add Greek yogurt for extra creaminess and blend again until well combined.
4. Season the dip with salt and pepper to taste. Adjust the consistency by adding more olive oil if needed.
5. Transfer the dip to a serving bowl and refrigerate for at least 30 minutes to allow the flavors to meld.
6. Before serving, garnish with a drizzle of olive oil, a sprinkle of Parmesan cheese, and a few fresh basil leaves.
7. Serve with an assortment of fresh vegetables and whole-grain crackers.

Nutrition Information:
Per serving (assuming 8 servings):
- Calories: 180, Total Fat: 12g, Saturated Fat: 2g, Trans Fat: 0g, Cholesterol: 3mg, Sodium: 150mg, Total Carbohydrates: 14g, Dietary Fiber: 3g, Sugars: 1g, Protein: 6g

Note: Nutrition Information may vary based on specific ingredients used and serving sizes.

10. Smoky Chipotle Butter Bean Dip

This Smoky Chipotle Butter Bean Dip is a delicious and nutritious twist on a classic dip. Butter beans, also known as lima beans, provide a creamy texture and a boost of protein, making this dip a healthy and satisfying option for snacking or entertaining. The smoky chipotle flavor adds a subtle kick, elevating the dip to a new level of taste. Pair it with fresh veggies, whole-grain crackers, or pita bread for a wholesome and flavorful treat.

Serving: 8 servings
Preparation Time: 15 minutes

Ready Time: 20 minutes

Ingredients:
- 2 cans (15 ounces each) butter beans, drained and rinsed
- 2 cloves garlic, minced
- 1 chipotle pepper in adobo sauce, minced (adjust to taste for spiciness)
- 2 tablespoons tahini
- 2 tablespoons olive oil
- 1 tablespoon fresh lemon juice
- 1 teaspoon ground cumin
- 1/2 teaspoon smoked paprika
- Salt and pepper to taste
- 2 tablespoons fresh cilantro, chopped (for garnish)

Instructions:
1. In a food processor, combine the butter beans, minced garlic, chipotle pepper, tahini, olive oil, lemon juice, cumin, smoked paprika, salt, and pepper.
2. Blend the ingredients until smooth and creamy, scraping down the sides of the processor as needed to ensure an even consistency.
3. Taste the dip and adjust the seasonings if necessary, adding more chipotle pepper for extra heat or lemon juice for brightness.
4. Transfer the dip to a serving bowl and garnish with fresh cilantro.
5. Serve the Smoky Chipotle Butter Bean Dip with a variety of dippables such as carrot sticks, cucumber slices, whole-grain crackers, or pita bread.

Nutrition Information
(per serving):
- Calories: 120, Total Fat: 6g, Saturated Fat: 1g, Trans Fat: 0g, Cholesterol: 0mg, Sodium: 180mg, Total Carbohydrates: 13g, Dietary Fiber: 4g, Sugars: 0g, Protein: 5g

Note: Nutrition Information is approximate and may vary based on specific ingredients used. Adjust quantities and ingredients according to dietary preferences and restrictions.

11. Butter Bean and Sun-Dried Tomato Tapenade

Indulge in the wholesome goodness of butter beans with this delightful Butter Bean and Sun-Dried Tomato Tapenade. Packed with protein, fiber, and a burst of Mediterranean flavors, this recipe is a testament to the versatility of butter beans in creating healthy and delicious dishes. The creamy texture of butter beans combines seamlessly with the intense sun-dried tomatoes, creating a tapenade that can be enjoyed as a spread, dip, or a flavorful topping.

Serving: Makes approximately 1.5 cups of tapenade.
Preparation Time: 15 minutes
Ready Time: 15 minutes

Ingredients:
- 1 can (15 ounces) butter beans, drained and rinsed
- 1/2 cup sun-dried tomatoes (not oil-packed), soaked in hot water for 10 minutes and drained
- 2 cloves garlic, minced
- 1/4 cup fresh basil leaves
- 2 tablespoons pine nuts, toasted
- 1/4 cup extra-virgin olive oil
- 1 tablespoon balsamic vinegar
- Salt and pepper to taste

Instructions:
1. In a food processor, combine the drained butter beans, rehydrated sun-dried tomatoes, minced garlic, fresh basil leaves, and toasted pine nuts.
2. Pulse the ingredients until they are roughly chopped.
3. With the food processor running, drizzle in the olive oil and balsamic vinegar until the mixture reaches your desired consistency. You can leave it slightly chunky for texture or process it more for a smoother tapenade.
4. Season with salt and pepper to taste, and pulse again to combine.
5. Transfer the tapenade to a serving bowl and refrigerate for at least 30 minutes to allow the flavors to meld.
6. Serve the Butter Bean and Sun-Dried Tomato Tapenade with whole-grain crackers, sliced baguette, or as a topping for grilled vegetables.

Nutrition Information:
Per Serving (2 tablespoons):

- Calories: 90, Total Fat: 7g, Saturated Fat: 1g, Trans Fat: 0g, Cholesterol: 0mg, Sodium: 120mg, Total Carbohydrates: 6g, Dietary Fiber: 2g, Sugars: 1g, Protein: 2g

This Butter Bean and Sun-Dried Tomato Tapenade not only tantalizes your taste buds but also offers a healthy dose of nutrients, making it a perfect addition to your collection of butter bean recipes.

12. Butter Bean and Feta Cheese Dip

Elevate your snacking experience with this nutritious and flavorful Butter Bean and Feta Cheese Dip. Packed with protein, fiber, and the rich creaminess of feta, this dip is a delightful twist on a classic favorite. Butter beans add a hearty texture and a boost of nutritional goodness, making it a perfect choice for a healthy snack or party appetizer. Prepare to indulge guilt-free in this simple yet delectable dip that celebrates the versatility of butter beans.

Serving: Ideal as a dip for fresh vegetables, whole-grain crackers, or pita chips. This recipe serves 6-8 people.
Preparation Time: 15 minutes
Ready Time: 15 minutes

Ingredients:
- 2 cans (15 ounces each) butter beans, drained and rinsed
- 1/2 cup crumbled feta cheese
- 1/4 cup plain Greek yogurt
- 2 tablespoons olive oil
- 1 tablespoon lemon juice
- 2 cloves garlic, minced
- 1 teaspoon ground cumin
- Salt and pepper to taste
- Fresh parsley for garnish (optional)

Instructions:
1. In a food processor, combine the butter beans, feta cheese, Greek yogurt, olive oil, lemon juice, minced garlic, and ground cumin.
2. Blend the mixture until smooth and creamy. If needed, add a splash of water to achieve your desired consistency.

3. Season with salt and pepper to taste, adjusting as necessary.
4. Transfer the dip to a serving bowl and garnish with fresh parsley if desired.
5. Serve the Butter Bean and Feta Cheese Dip with an array of colorful vegetable sticks, whole-grain crackers, or pita chips.

Nutrition Information:
Note: Nutrition Information is approximate and may vary based on specific ingredients used and portion sizes.
- Serving Size: 1/4 cup
- Calories: 120, Total Fat: 7g, Saturated Fat: 2g, Trans Fat: 0g, Cholesterol: 10mg, Sodium: 200mg, Total Carbohydrates: 11g, Dietary Fiber: 3g, Sugars: 1g, Protein: 5g

Indulge in the wholesome goodness of this Butter Bean and Feta Cheese Dip, a delightful addition to your repertoire of healthy and flavorful recipes. Perfect for gatherings or solo snacking, this dip will become a favorite for its balance of creamy textures and vibrant flavors.

13. Creamy Butter Bean and Roasted Garlic Dip

Indulge your taste buds in the delightful fusion of wholesome flavors with our Creamy Butter Bean and Roasted Garlic Dip. This appetizing dip not only elevates the humble butter bean but also provides a healthy alternative to traditional dips. The rich, creamy texture is complemented by the earthy essence of roasted garlic, creating a versatile dip that can be paired with crisp veggies, whole-grain crackers, or used as a spread for sandwiches. Packed with protein and fiber, this recipe embodies the essence of our cookbook, "Healthy Ways to Use Butter Beans," making it a perfect addition to your repertoire of nutritious and delicious dishes.

Serving: Ideal for 6-8 servings.
Preparation Time: 15 minutes
Ready Time: 40 minutes

Ingredients:
- 2 cans (15 ounces each) butter beans, drained and rinsed
- 1 head of garlic
- 2 tablespoons olive oil

- 1/4 cup tahini
- 1/4 cup Greek yogurt
- 2 tablespoons fresh lemon juice
- 1 teaspoon ground cumin
- Salt and pepper, to taste
- Fresh parsley, for garnish (optional)
- Whole-grain crackers or vegetable sticks, for serving

Instructions:
1. Roast the Garlic:
- Preheat the oven to 400°F (200°C).
- Slice off the top of the garlic head to expose the cloves.
- Place the garlic on a piece of aluminum foil, drizzle with olive oil, and wrap it securely.
- Roast in the preheated oven for 30-35 minutes or until the garlic cloves are soft and golden. Allow it to cool.
2. Prepare the Butter Beans:
- In a food processor, combine the butter beans, tahini, Greek yogurt, lemon juice, cumin, and the roasted garlic cloves (squeezed from the skin).
- Blend until smooth and creamy, scraping down the sides as needed.
3. Season and Garnish:
- Season the dip with salt and pepper to taste, adjusting as needed.
- If desired, garnish with fresh parsley for a burst of color and added freshness.
4. Serve:
- Transfer the creamy butter bean and roasted garlic dip to a serving bowl.
- Serve with whole-grain crackers or an assortment of vegetable sticks for a wholesome and satisfying snack or appetizer.

Nutrition Information:
Note: Nutrition Information is approximate and may vary based on specific ingredients and serving sizes.
- Serving Size: 1/4 cup
- Calories: 120, Total Fat: 7g, Saturated Fat: 1g, Cholesterol: 1mg, Sodium: 150mg, Total Carbohydrates: 11g, Dietary Fiber: 3g, Sugars: 1g, Protein: 5g

Indulge in this Creamy Butter Bean and Roasted Garlic Dip guilt-free, as it not only satisfies your taste buds but also contributes to your well-being. Enjoy the delightful journey of flavors with every wholesome bite.

14. Thai-Inspired Butter Bean Dip

Indulge your taste buds in the vibrant flavors of Thailand with this delectable Thai-Inspired Butter Bean Dip. Butter beans, also known as lima beans, take center stage in this healthy and flavorful recipe. Packed with protein, fiber, and a medley of Thai-inspired herbs and spices, this dip is not only delicious but also a nutritious addition to your snack or appetizer repertoire. Get ready to elevate your culinary experience with this exotic twist on a classic dip!

Serving: Ideal for 6-8 servings
Preparation Time: 15 minutes
Ready Time: 20 minutes

Ingredients:
- 2 cans (15 ounces each) butter beans, drained and rinsed
- 1/4 cup tahini
- 2 tablespoons fresh lime juice
- 2 tablespoons soy sauce
- 1 tablespoon sesame oil
- 2 cloves garlic, minced
- 1 teaspoon grated fresh ginger
- 1 teaspoon honey or maple syrup (optional for sweetness)
- 1/2 teaspoon ground cumin
- 1/2 teaspoon red pepper flakes (adjust to taste)
- 2 tablespoons chopped fresh cilantro
- 2 green onions, finely sliced
- Salt and pepper to taste
- Sesame seeds for garnish

Instructions:
1. In a food processor, combine the butter beans, tahini, lime juice, soy sauce, sesame oil, garlic, ginger, honey (if using), cumin, and red pepper flakes. Blend until smooth and creamy.

2. Taste the dip and adjust the seasoning with salt and pepper as needed.
3. Add the chopped cilantro and green onions to the mixture, pulsing a few times to incorporate them into the dip while maintaining some texture.
4. Transfer the dip to a serving bowl, drizzle with a bit of extra sesame oil, and garnish with sesame seeds.
5. Serve the Thai-Inspired Butter Bean Dip with an array of fresh vegetables, pita chips, or whole-grain crackers.

Nutrition Information:
(Per serving - based on 6 servings)
- Calories: 180, Protein: 7g, Fat: 8g, Carbohydrates: 21g, Fiber: 6g, Sugar: 2g, Sodium: 400mg
Savor the exotic taste of Thailand with this nutritious and flavorful dip. Perfect for entertaining or a healthy snack, this Thai-inspired butter bean dip is sure to become a favorite in your repertoire of wholesome recipes. Enjoy the fusion of health and taste in every bite!

15. Butter Bean and Spinach Dip

Elevate your snack game with this nutritious and delicious Butter Bean and Spinach Dip. Packed with protein-rich butter beans and vibrant spinach, this dip is a wholesome twist on a classic favorite. It's perfect for parties, picnics, or simply as a guilt-free indulgence. Get ready to savor the creamy goodness and nourish your body with every bite.

Serving: Makes approximately 2 cups of dip.
Preparation Time: 15 minutes
Ready Time: 30 minutes

Ingredients:
- 1 can (15 ounces) butter beans, drained and rinsed
- 2 cups fresh spinach leaves, chopped
- 1/4 cup plain Greek yogurt
- 2 tablespoons olive oil
- 2 cloves garlic, minced
- 1 tablespoon lemon juice
- 1/2 teaspoon cumin

- 1/2 teaspoon paprika
- Salt and pepper to taste
- 1/4 cup feta cheese, crumbled (optional, for garnish)
- Fresh parsley, chopped (optional, for garnish)
- Assorted vegetables and whole-grain crackers for serving

Instructions:
1. In a food processor, combine the butter beans, chopped spinach, Greek yogurt, olive oil, minced garlic, lemon juice, cumin, paprika, salt, and pepper.
2. Process the mixture until smooth and creamy, scraping down the sides as needed.
3. Taste and adjust the seasonings if necessary.
4. Transfer the dip to a serving bowl and refrigerate for at least 15 minutes to allow the flavors to meld.
5. Before serving, garnish with crumbled feta cheese and chopped fresh parsley if desired.
6. Serve the Butter Bean and Spinach Dip with an assortment of fresh vegetables and whole-grain crackers.

Nutrition Information:
(Per 2-tablespoon serving)
- Calories: 60, Protein: 3g, Carbohydrates: 7g, Fiber: 2g, Sugars: 1g, Fat: 3g, Saturated Fat: 1g, Cholesterol: 3mg, Sodium: 80mg

Enjoy this nutritious and flavorful dip guilt-free, knowing that each bite is contributing to your well-being. It's a versatile and satisfying addition to your repertoire of healthy butter bean recipes.

16. Butter Bean and Cilantro Hummus

This Butter Bean and Cilantro Hummus recipe offers a delightful twist to the classic hummus, infusing the creamy texture of butter beans with the vibrant freshness of cilantro. It's a nutritious, protein-packed dip perfect for snacking or as a spread on sandwiches and wraps. Embrace a healthier alternative without compromising on flavor!
 Serving:
Serves 6-8
 Preparation time:

15 minutes
Ready time:
15 minutes

Ingredients:
- 2 cans (15 ounces each) butter beans, drained and rinsed
- 1/4 cup tahini
- 1/4 cup fresh cilantro leaves, chopped
- 2 cloves garlic, minced
- 3 tablespoons fresh lemon juice
- 2 tablespoons extra-virgin olive oil
- 1/2 teaspoon ground cumin
- Salt and pepper to taste
- Optional: Paprika or additional olive oil for garnish

Instructions:
1. In a food processor, combine the butter beans, tahini, cilantro, minced garlic, lemon juice, olive oil, cumin, salt, and pepper.
2. Blend the ingredients until smooth and creamy, scraping down the sides of the processor as needed to ensure everything is well combined.
3. Taste the hummus and adjust seasonings if necessary, adding more salt, pepper, or lemon juice to suit your preference.
4. Transfer the hummus to a serving bowl. If desired, drizzle a bit of olive oil over the top and sprinkle with paprika for an extra touch of flavor and presentation.
5. Serve the butter bean and cilantro hummus with fresh vegetable sticks, pita bread, or use as a spread on sandwiches.

Nutrition Information:
Note: Nutritional values are approximate and may vary based on ingredients used.
- Serving Size: 1/4 cup
- Calories: 120, Total Fat: 6g, Saturated Fat: 1g, Sodium: 180mg, Total Carbohydrates: 13g, Dietary Fiber: 3g, Sugars: 0g, Protein: 4g

Enjoy this nutritious and flavorful butter bean and cilantro hummus as a guilt-free snack or accompaniment to your favorite dishes!

17. Roasted Eggplant and Butter Bean Dip

This Roasted Eggplant and Butter Bean Dip is a delightful blend of smoky eggplant, creamy butter beans, and zesty flavors. Packed with nutrients and protein, it's a perfect addition to your healthy eating routine. Whether as a snack or a party dip, its velvety texture and rich taste will surely impress.

Serving:
Serves: 6-8
Preparation time:
Prep: 15 minutes
Ready time:
Total: 45 minutes

Ingredients:
- 1 large eggplant
- 1 can (15 oz) butter beans, drained and rinsed
- 2 cloves garlic, minced
- 2 tablespoons tahini
- 2 tablespoons lemon juice
- 2 tablespoons extra-virgin olive oil
- 1 teaspoon ground cumin
- 1/2 teaspoon smoked paprika
- Salt and pepper to taste
- Fresh parsley, chopped (for garnish)
- Optional: Red pepper flakes for a hint of spice

Instructions:
1. Preheat the oven to 400°F (200°C).
2. Pierce the eggplant several times with a fork and place it on a baking sheet lined with parchment paper. Roast in the oven for 30-35 minutes, or until the skin is charred, and the eggplant is soft.
3. Remove the eggplant from the oven and let it cool for a few minutes. Once cool enough to handle, peel off the skin and roughly chop the flesh.
4. In a food processor or blender, combine the roasted eggplant, drained butter beans, minced garlic, tahini, lemon juice, olive oil, ground cumin, smoked paprika, salt, and pepper.

5. Blend the mixture until smooth and creamy, scraping down the sides as needed. Adjust seasonings to taste, adding more lemon juice or spices if desired.

6. Transfer the dip to a serving bowl. Drizzle with a bit of olive oil and sprinkle chopped parsley on top for garnish. If you like it spicy, add a pinch of red pepper flakes.

7. Serve the dip with your choice of fresh vegetables, pita bread, or whole-grain crackers.

Nutrition Information:
- Calories: Approximately 120 per serving, Total Fat: 7g, Saturated Fat: 1g, Cholesterol: 0mg, Sodium: 150mg, Total Carbohydrates: 12g, Dietary Fiber: 4g
- Total Sugars: 2g, Protein: 4g

Nutritional values may vary based on specific ingredients used. Enjoy this flavorful dip as a nutritious addition to your meals or as a crowd-pleasing appetizer!

18. Sweet Potato and Butter Bean Hummus

This vibrant and nutritious Sweet Potato and Butter Bean Hummus recipe is a delightful twist on the classic hummus, infusing it with the earthy sweetness of sweet potatoes and the creamy richness of butter beans. Packed with protein, fiber, and essential nutrients, it's a wholesome dip that elevates any snack or meal.

Serving: Makes about 2 cups of hummus
Preparation time: 15 minutes
Ready time: 45 minutes

Ingredients:
- 1 medium sweet potato, peeled and cubed
- 1 can (15 oz) butter beans, drained and rinsed
- 2 tablespoons tahini
- 2 cloves garlic, minced
- 2 tablespoons olive oil
- 2 tablespoons freshly squeezed lemon juice
- 1 teaspoon ground cumin

- 1/2 teaspoon smoked paprika
- Salt and pepper to taste
- Optional toppings: drizzle of olive oil, sprinkle of paprika, chopped fresh herbs

Instructions:
1. Preheat the oven to 400°F (200°C). Place the cubed sweet potato on a baking sheet lined with parchment paper. Drizzle with a bit of olive oil and sprinkle with salt and pepper. Roast for 25-30 minutes or until the sweet potato is tender and slightly caramelized. Let it cool for a few minutes.
2. In a food processor, combine the roasted sweet potato, butter beans, tahini, minced garlic, olive oil, lemon juice, cumin, smoked paprika, salt, and pepper.
3. Blend the ingredients until smooth and creamy, scraping down the sides of the processor as needed. If the consistency is too thick, add a tablespoon of water at a time until desired consistency is reached.
4. Taste and adjust the seasonings, adding more salt, pepper, or lemon juice if needed.
5. Transfer the sweet potato and butter bean hummus to a serving bowl. Drizzle with a bit of olive oil and sprinkle with paprika for an extra touch of flavor. Garnish with chopped fresh herbs if desired.

Nutrition Information
(per 2-tablespoon serving):
- Calories: 60, Total Fat: 3.5g, Saturated Fat: 0.5g, Sodium: 70mg, Total Carbohydrates: 5g, Dietary Fiber: 1g, Sugars: 0.5g, Protein: 2g
Nutritional values are approximate and may vary based on specific ingredients used.

19. Butter Bean and Walnut Dip

Elevate your snack game with this nutritious and flavorful Butter Bean and Walnut Dip. Packed with protein, fiber, and healthy fats, this dip not only satisfies your taste buds but also nourishes your body. Butter beans provide a creamy base, while walnuts add a delightful crunch and a dose of omega-3 fatty acids. Enjoy this wholesome dip as a spread on whole-grain crackers, vegetable sticks, or as a sandwich filling. It's a delightful addition to your repertoire of healthy recipes.

Serving: Makes approximately 2 cups of dip.
Preparation Time: 15 minutes
Ready Time: 15 minutes

Ingredients:
- 1 can (15 ounces) butter beans, drained and rinsed
- 1/2 cup walnuts, toasted
- 2 cloves garlic, minced
- 2 tablespoons fresh lemon juice
- 2 tablespoons extra-virgin olive oil
- 1 teaspoon ground cumin
- 1/2 teaspoon paprika
- Salt and pepper to taste
- 2 tablespoons fresh parsley, chopped (for garnish)

Instructions:
1. In a food processor, combine the butter beans, toasted walnuts, minced garlic, fresh lemon juice, extra-virgin olive oil, ground cumin, paprika, salt, and pepper.
2. Process the mixture until smooth and creamy. If the dip is too thick, you can add a little water or more olive oil to reach your desired consistency.
3. Taste the dip and adjust the seasoning if needed, adding more salt, pepper, or lemon juice to suit your preferences.
4. Transfer the dip to a serving bowl and garnish with fresh chopped parsley.
5. Serve the Butter Bean and Walnut Dip with whole-grain crackers, sliced vegetables, or as a spread in sandwiches.

Nutrition Information:
Note: Nutrition Information is approximate and may vary based on specific ingredients and serving sizes.
- Calories: 120 per 1/4 cup serving, Protein: 5g, Fat: 8g, Saturated Fat: 1g
- Monounsaturated Fat: 5g
- Polyunsaturated Fat: 2g, Carbohydrates: 10g, Fiber: 3g, Sugar: 1g, Cholesterol: 0mg, Sodium: 180mg

This Butter Bean and Walnut Dip is a delicious and wholesome alternative for those seeking healthy and satisfying snack options. Enjoy the rich flavors and nourishing goodness of this dip on any occasion.

20. Spiced Pumpkin Butter Bean Dip

Elevate your culinary experience with this delectable and nutritious Spiced Pumpkin Butter Bean Dip. Bursting with flavors and goodness, this dip is a perfect addition to your repertoire of healthy recipes. Butter beans, known for their creaminess and protein content, blend seamlessly with the rich, spiced pumpkin to create a dip that is both satisfying and wholesome. Whether you're entertaining guests or enjoying a cozy night in, this dip is a delightful choice that will leave everyone asking for more.

Serving: Serve the Spiced Pumpkin Butter Bean Dip as a delightful appetizer or snack. Pair it with whole-grain crackers, vegetable sticks, or pita bread for a satisfying and wholesome treat.
Preparation Time: 15 minutes
Ready Time: 25 minutes

Ingredients:
- 1 can (15 oz) butter beans, drained and rinsed
- 1 cup canned pumpkin puree
- 2 tablespoons tahini
- 2 cloves garlic, minced
- 1 teaspoon ground cumin
- 1/2 teaspoon ground coriander
- 1/2 teaspoon smoked paprika
- 1/4 teaspoon cayenne pepper (adjust to taste)
- Salt and black pepper to taste
- 2 tablespoons olive oil
- 2 tablespoons fresh lemon juice
- 2 tablespoons water (adjust for desired consistency)

Instructions:
1. In a food processor, combine the butter beans, pumpkin puree, tahini, minced garlic, cumin, coriander, smoked paprika, cayenne pepper, salt, and black pepper.

2. Pulse the ingredients until well combined and slightly smooth.
3. With the food processor running, drizzle in the olive oil and lemon juice. Continue to process until the dip reaches a creamy and smooth consistency.
4. If needed, add water gradually until the dip reaches your desired thickness.
5. Taste the dip and adjust the seasoning, adding more salt, pepper, or cayenne pepper according to your preference.
6. Transfer the Spiced Pumpkin Butter Bean Dip to a serving bowl.
7. Optionally, drizzle with a bit of olive oil and sprinkle with additional smoked paprika for garnish.
8. Serve the dip with your choice of accompaniments like whole-grain crackers, vegetable sticks, or pita bread.

Nutrition Information:
Note: Nutrition Information is approximate and may vary based on specific ingredients and serving sizes.
- Serving Size: 2 tablespoons
- Calories: 60, Total Fat: 4g, Saturated Fat: 0.5g, Cholesterol: 0mg, Sodium: 90mg, Total Carbohydrates: 6g, Dietary Fiber: 2g, Sugars: 1g, Protein: 2g

Enjoy this Spiced Pumpkin Butter Bean Dip as a flavorful and healthful addition to your meals. It's not just a dip; it's a culinary journey into wholesome indulgence.

21. Curried Butter Bean Dip

This delightful Curried Butter Bean Dip offers a fusion of flavors that elevate the humble butter beans to a new level. Packed with protein and fiber, this recipe presents a healthy and versatile option perfect for snacks, spreads, or a side dish. Its aromatic spices and creamy texture make it a crowd-pleaser at gatherings or a delightful addition to your everyday meals.

Serving:
Serves: 6-8 people
Preparation time:
Prep: 10 minutes
Ready time:

Ready in: 15 minutes

Ingredients:
- 2 cans (15 oz each) butter beans, drained and rinsed
- 2 tablespoons olive oil
- 1 small onion, finely chopped
- 2 cloves garlic, minced
- 1 teaspoon curry powder
- 1/2 teaspoon ground cumin
- 1/2 teaspoon ground coriander
- 1/4 teaspoon turmeric
- 1/4 teaspoon cayenne pepper (adjust to taste)
- Juice of 1 lemon
- Salt and pepper to taste
- 2 tablespoons chopped fresh cilantro (optional, for garnish)

Instructions:
1. Heat olive oil in a skillet over medium heat. Add the chopped onion and sauté until translucent, about 3-4 minutes.
2. Add minced garlic to the skillet and cook for an additional minute until fragrant.
3. Stir in the curry powder, cumin, coriander, turmeric, and cayenne pepper. Cook the spices with the onions and garlic for about a minute to release their flavors.
4. Add the drained and rinsed butter beans to the skillet, stirring to combine and heat through, about 2-3 minutes.
5. Transfer the mixture to a food processor. Add lemon juice, salt, and pepper. Blend until smooth and creamy. If needed, adjust seasoning to taste.
6. Garnish with chopped cilantro if desired.
7. Serve the Curried Butter Bean Dip with pita bread, vegetable sticks, or your favorite crackers.

Nutrition Information:
(Per serving, based on 6 servings)
- Calories: 180, Total Fat: 6g, Saturated Fat: 1g, Trans Fat: 0g, Cholesterol: 0mg, Sodium: 290mg
- Total Carbohydrate: 25g, Dietary Fiber: 7g, Sugars: 2g, Protein: 8g

Nutritional values are approximate and may vary depending on ingredients used.
This Curried Butter Bean Dip not only boasts incredible flavors but also provides a healthy dose of nutrients, making it a fantastic addition to your menu. Enjoy its creamy texture and aromatic spices while indulging in a guilt-free snack or accompaniment to your meals.

22. Black Olive and Butter Bean Tapenade

Indulge in the exquisite flavors of the Mediterranean with our Black Olive and Butter Bean Tapenade—a delightful fusion of buttery beans and briny olives. This recipe not only captivates the taste buds but also celebrates the nutritional benefits of butter beans, offering a healthy twist to a classic tapenade. Elevate your culinary experience with this simple and nutritious dish that can be enjoyed as a spread, dip, or a flavorful topping.
Serving: 8 servings
Preparation time: 15 minutes
Ready time: 15 minutes

Ingredients:
- 1 can (15 oz) butter beans, drained and rinsed
- 1 cup pitted black olives
- 2 cloves garlic, minced
- 2 tablespoons capers, drained
- 1/4 cup fresh parsley, chopped
- 2 tablespoons fresh lemon juice
- 1/3 cup extra virgin olive oil
- Salt and pepper to taste

Instructions:
1. In a food processor, combine the butter beans, black olives, minced garlic, capers, and fresh parsley.
2. Pulse the mixture until coarsely chopped, ensuring a textured consistency.
3. While the processor is running, slowly drizzle in the extra virgin olive oil until the tapenade reaches a smooth, spreadable consistency.

4. Add fresh lemon juice, salt, and pepper to taste, and pulse once more to combine.
5. Taste and adjust seasonings if necessary, balancing the flavors to your liking.
6. Transfer the tapenade to a serving bowl and refrigerate for at least 30 minutes to allow the flavors to meld.
7. Before serving, let the tapenade come to room temperature for optimal taste.
8. Serve with whole-grain crackers, toasted baguette slices, or fresh vegetable sticks.

Nutrition Information
(per serving):
- Calories: 150, Total Fat: 11g, Saturated Fat: 1.5g, Trans Fat: 0g, Cholesterol: 0mg, Sodium: 400mg, Total Carbohydrates: 11g, Dietary Fiber: 3g, Sugars: 1g, Protein: 3g
- Vitamin D: 0%
- Calcium: 4%
- Iron: 6%
- Potassium: 4%

Enjoy the harmonious blend of textures and flavors in this Black Olive and Butter Bean Tapenade—a perfect addition to your repertoire of healthy and delicious recipes.

23. Butter Bean and Roasted Red Onion Dip

Elevate your snacking experience with this nutritious and flavorful Butter Bean and Roasted Red Onion Dip. Packed with protein, fiber, and essential nutrients, butter beans take center stage in this deliciously wholesome recipe. The addition of roasted red onions adds a sweet and savory depth, making this dip a perfect companion for fresh veggies or whole-grain crackers. It's a delightful way to incorporate the goodness of butter beans into your diet, proving that healthy can also be incredibly tasty!

Serving: Serves 6-8
Preparation Time: 15 minutes
Ready Time: 45 minutes

Ingredients:
- 2 cans (15 ounces each) butter beans, drained and rinsed
- 1 large red onion, thinly sliced
- 2 cloves garlic, minced
- 2 tablespoons olive oil
- 1 teaspoon cumin
- 1 teaspoon smoked paprika
- Salt and pepper to taste
- Juice of 1 lemon
- 2 tablespoons fresh parsley, chopped (for garnish)

Instructions:
1. Preheat the Oven: Preheat your oven to 400°F (200°C).
2. Roast the Red Onion: In a baking dish, toss the sliced red onion with 1 tablespoon of olive oil. Roast in the preheated oven for 20-25 minutes or until the onions are caramelized and golden brown.
3. Prepare the Butter Beans: In a food processor, combine the butter beans, roasted red onions, minced garlic, cumin, smoked paprika, salt, and pepper.
4. Blend: Pulse the ingredients until smooth. While blending, drizzle in the remaining olive oil and add lemon juice. Continue to blend until the dip reaches a creamy consistency.
5. Adjust Seasoning: Taste the dip and adjust the seasoning, if necessary, by adding more salt, pepper, or lemon juice.
6. Serve: Transfer the dip to a serving bowl, garnish with chopped parsley, and serve with your favorite fresh vegetables or whole-grain crackers.

Nutrition Information:
(Per Serving - Based on 6 servings)
- Calories: 180, Protein: 7g, Carbohydrates: 26g, Fiber: 7g, Fat: 6g, Saturated Fat: 1g, Cholesterol: 0mg, Sodium: 300mg

Enjoy this Butter Bean and Roasted Red Onion Dip as a wholesome snack or appetizer, and feel good about nourishing your body with the goodness of butter beans!

24. Butter Bean and Roasted Beet Hummus

Embrace the wholesome goodness of butter beans with this vibrant and nutritious Butter Bean and Roasted Beet Hummus recipe. Elevate your snacking experience with a colorful twist that not only tantalizes your taste buds but also packs a punch of health benefits. The creamy texture of butter beans pairs perfectly with the earthy sweetness of roasted beets, creating a hummus that's as visually appealing as it is delicious. Get ready to indulge in a guilt-free treat that celebrates the versatility of butter beans in a uniquely delightful way.

Serving: Makes approximately 2 cups of hummus.
Preparation Time: 15 minutes
Ready Time: 45 minutes (includes roasting time for beets)

Ingredients:
- 1 can (15 ounces) butter beans, drained and rinsed
- 2 medium-sized beets, roasted, peeled, and chopped
- 3 tablespoons tahini
- 2 cloves garlic, minced
- 1/4 cup fresh lemon juice
- 1/4 cup extra-virgin olive oil, plus extra for drizzling
- 1 teaspoon ground cumin
- Salt and pepper to taste
- Water (as needed for desired consistency)
- Optional garnish: chopped fresh parsley and a sprinkle of sesame seeds

Instructions:
1. Roast the Beets:
- Preheat the oven to 400°F (200°C).
- Wrap each beet in aluminum foil and place them on a baking sheet.
- Roast for approximately 40 minutes or until the beets are tender.
- Allow the beets to cool, then peel and chop them into smaller pieces.
2. Prepare the Hummus:
- In a food processor, combine the butter beans, roasted beets, tahini, minced garlic, lemon juice, olive oil, cumin, salt, and pepper.
- Blend until smooth, stopping to scrape down the sides as needed.
- If the hummus is too thick, add water a tablespoon at a time until you reach your desired consistency.
3. Adjust Seasoning:

- Taste the hummus and adjust the seasoning, adding more salt, pepper, or lemon juice as needed.
4. Serve:
- Transfer the hummus to a serving bowl.
- Drizzle with extra olive oil and garnish with chopped fresh parsley and sesame seeds if desired.
5.

Nutrition Information:
- (Per 2-tablespoon serving)
- Calories: 80, Protein: 2g, Carbohydrates: 7g, Dietary Fiber: 2g, Sugars: 1g, Fat: 5g, Saturated Fat: 1g, Cholesterol: 0mg, Sodium: 70mg

Indulge in this Butter Bean and Roasted Beet Hummus as a nutritious dip, spread, or topping for your favorite dishes. This vibrant and flavorful creation is not just a treat for your taste buds but also a celebration of the health benefits tucked away in every butter bean. Enjoy the journey to a healthier you with this delightful recipe!

25. Butter Bean and Caramelized Onion Dip

Creamy, savory, and brimming with wholesome flavors, this Butter Bean and Caramelized Onion Dip is a delightful spin on a classic favorite. Butter beans, known for their velvety texture and nutty taste, take center stage in this nutritious dip. Combined with the sweetness of caramelized onions and a medley of herbs, it's a perfect blend for your snacking pleasure. Versatile and simple to make, this dip is a must-have for gatherings or as a flavorful addition to your everyday spread.

Serving: Makes about 2 cups of dip
Preparation time: 15 minutes
Ready time: 45 minutes

Ingredients:
- 2 cups cooked butter beans (canned or soaked and boiled)
- 2 large onions, thinly sliced
- 2 cloves garlic, minced
- 2 tablespoons olive oil
- 1 tablespoon balsamic vinegar
- 1 teaspoon dried thyme

- 1 teaspoon paprika
- Salt and black pepper to taste
- 2 tablespoons fresh parsley, chopped (for garnish, optional)

Instructions:
1. Caramelize the Onions: Heat olive oil in a skillet over medium heat. Add the thinly sliced onions and sauté until they start to soften, about 5 minutes.
2. Reduce the heat to low-medium. Continue cooking the onions, stirring occasionally, for about 30 minutes until they turn golden brown and caramelized.
3. Add minced garlic, balsamic vinegar, thyme, paprika, salt, and black pepper to the caramelized onions. Cook for an additional 3-4 minutes until fragrant. Remove from heat and let it cool slightly.
4. In a food processor, combine the cooked butter beans and the caramelized onion mixture. Blend until smooth and creamy. If needed, add a splash of water or olive oil to achieve the desired consistency.
5. Transfer the dip to a serving bowl. Garnish with chopped fresh parsley, if desired.
6. Serve the Butter Bean and Caramelized Onion Dip with your choice of veggies, pita chips, or crackers.

Nutrition Information
(per 2 tablespoons):
- Calories: 50, Total Fat: 2g, Saturated Fat: 0.3g, Cholesterol: 0mg, Sodium: 65mg
- Total Carbohydrate: 7g, Dietary Fiber: 2g, Sugars: 1g, Protein: 2g
Nutritional values are approximate and may vary based on specific ingredients used.

26. Creamy Butter Bean and Dill Dip

Butter beans, with their creamy texture and mild flavor, are a versatile legume perfect for creating wholesome yet delicious dishes. This Creamy Butter Bean and Dill Dip offers a delightful blend of flavors, combining the richness of butter beans with the freshness of dill. Enjoy it as a nutritious dip or spread that's both satisfying and healthy.
Serving: Makes approximately 2 cups of dip

Preparation time: 10 minutes
Ready time: 10 minutes

Ingredients:
- 2 cans (15 ounces each) butter beans, drained and rinsed
- 2 cloves garlic, minced
- 2 tablespoons fresh dill, chopped
- 2 tablespoons lemon juice
- 1/4 cup olive oil
- Salt and pepper to taste
- Optional: 2 tablespoons Greek yogurt or sour cream for added creaminess

Instructions:
1. In a food processor, combine the drained and rinsed butter beans, minced garlic, fresh dill, and lemon juice.
2. Pulse the mixture a few times to start breaking down the beans.
3. While the processor is running, gradually add the olive oil in a steady stream until the dip reaches a creamy consistency.
4. Season with salt and pepper to taste. Adjust the flavors by adding more lemon juice or dill if desired.
5. For extra creaminess, blend in Greek yogurt or sour cream if using.
6. Transfer the dip to a serving bowl and garnish with a sprig of dill.
7. Serve the Creamy Butter Bean and Dill Dip with your favorite veggies, pita chips, or crackers.

Nutrition Information
(per 2 tablespoons):
- Calories: 60, Total Fat: 3.5g, Saturated Fat: 0.5g, Cholesterol: 0mg, Sodium: 115mg, Total Carbohydrates: 5g, Dietary Fiber: 1.5g, Sugars: 0.5g, Protein: 2g

This nutrient-packed dip is not only a flavorful addition to any meal or snack but also a great source of plant-based protein and fiber, making it a healthy choice for all occasions.

27. Butter Bean and Smoked Paprika Dip

Butter Bean and Smoked Paprika Dip

Embrace the creamy richness of butter beans with a touch of smoky warmth from paprika in this delightful dip. Perfect for those looking to add a nutritious yet flavorful element to their appetizer spread or as a healthy snack accompaniment. Not only does this dip satisfy the taste buds, but it also packs in essential nutrients, making it a must-have in your culinary repertoire.

Serving: Makes approximately 2 cups of dip.
Preparation Time: 10 minutes.
Ready Time: 15 minutes.

Ingredients:
1. 2 cups cooked butter beans (canned beans, drained and rinsed, can be used)
2. 2 garlic cloves, minced
3. 2 tablespoons tahini (sesame seed paste)
4. Juice of 1 lemon
5. 1 teaspoon smoked paprika, plus extra for garnish
6. 3 tablespoons extra virgin olive oil
7. Salt, to taste
8. 2-3 tablespoons water (adjust based on desired consistency)
9. Fresh parsley, chopped (for garnish, optional)

Instructions:
1. Preparation: Start by ensuring your butter beans are well-drained and rinsed if using canned ones.
2. Blend: In a food processor or blender, combine the butter beans, minced garlic, tahini, lemon juice, smoked paprika, and salt.
3. Blend Again: While blending, slowly drizzle in the olive oil and continue to blend until you achieve a smooth and creamy consistency. If the dip seems too thick, add water, one tablespoon at a time, until desired consistency is reached.
4. Taste and Adjust: Taste the dip and adjust seasoning if necessary. If you desire more smokiness, add an extra pinch of smoked paprika and blend briefly.
5. Serve: Transfer the butter bean and smoked paprika dip to a serving bowl. Drizzle a little extra virgin olive oil on top and sprinkle with some smoked paprika and chopped parsley for garnish.

6. Enjoy: Serve the dip with fresh vegetables, pita bread, or whole-grain crackers. Store any leftovers in an airtight container in the refrigerator for up to 3-4 days.

Nutrition Information
(per 2 tablespoons serving):
- Calories: 60, Total Fat: 4g, Saturated Fat: 0.5g, Trans Fat: 0g, Cholesterol: 0mg, Sodium: 60mg, Total Carbohydrates: 5g, Dietary Fiber: 1g, Sugars: 0.5g, Protein: 2g
Note: Nutrition Information is approximate and may vary based on specific ingredients used and serving sizes.

28. Roasted Carrot and Butter Bean Hummus

Dive into the wholesome flavors of roasted carrots combined with creamy butter beans in this delightful hummus recipe. Not only does this dish offer a vibrant color and delightful taste, but it also packs a nutritious punch. Butter beans, rich in protein and fiber, blend seamlessly with the sweetness of roasted carrots, creating a creamy and flavorful hummus that's perfect for spreading, dipping, or enjoying on its own. Whether you're looking for a nutritious snack, appetizer, or a flavorful addition to your meals, this Roasted Carrot and Butter Bean Hummus is sure to please both your taste buds and your health goals.
 Serving:
Makes approximately 2 cups of hummus.
 Preparation Time:
15 minutes
 Ready Time:
45 minutes

Ingredients:
- 3 medium-sized carrots, peeled and cut into 1-inch pieces
- 1 can (15 ounces) butter beans, drained and rinsed
- 3 cloves garlic, minced
- 3 tablespoons tahini
- 2 tablespoons lemon juice
- 2 tablespoons olive oil, plus extra for roasting
- 1 teaspoon ground cumin

- ½ teaspoon paprika
- Salt and pepper to taste
- 2-4 tablespoons water (as needed for desired consistency)
- Fresh parsley or cilantro, for garnish (optional)

Instructions:
1. Preheat the Oven: Preheat your oven to 400°F (200°C).
2. Roast the Carrots: Place the carrot pieces on a baking sheet. Drizzle with olive oil, sprinkle with a pinch of salt and pepper, and toss to coat. Roast in the preheated oven for about 25-30 minutes or until the carrots are tender and slightly caramelized. Remove from the oven and let them cool slightly.
3. Prepare the Hummus Base: In a food processor, combine the roasted carrots, butter beans, minced garlic, tahini, lemon juice, olive oil, ground cumin, paprika, salt, and pepper.
4. Blend Until Smooth: Pulse the mixture until it starts to blend, then gradually add 2-4 tablespoons of water, one tablespoon at a time, until you achieve a smooth and creamy consistency. Scrape down the sides of the food processor as needed to ensure everything is well combined.
5. Taste and Adjust: Taste the hummus and adjust the seasoning if necessary. If you prefer a thinner consistency, you can add a bit more water or olive oil and blend again.
6. Serve and Garnish: Transfer the Roasted Carrot and Butter Bean Hummus to a serving dish. Drizzle with a bit of olive oil and garnish with fresh parsley or cilantro if desired. Serve with your favorite crackers, sliced vegetables, or pita bread.

Nutrition Information
(per 2 tablespoons):
- Calories: 60, Total Fat: 3.5g, Saturated Fat: 0.5g, Trans Fat: 0g, Cholesterol: 0mg, Sodium: 70mg, Total Carbohydrates: 6g, Dietary Fiber: 1.5g, Sugars: 1g, Protein: 2g

Note: Nutrition Information is an estimate and may vary based on the specific ingredients used.

29. Butter Bean and Sunflower Seed Dip

Butter Bean and Sunflower Seed Dip

Dive into the creamy goodness of this Butter Bean and Sunflower Seed Dip. A delightful fusion that brings together the earthy flavors of butter beans with the nuttiness of sunflower seeds. This dip is not only scrumptious but also packed with protein and essential nutrients. Perfect for spreading on crackers, dipping veggies, or even as a sandwich spread, it's a versatile addition to any table!

Serving: Makes about 2 cups of dip.
Preparation Time: 15 minutes
Ready Time: 20 minutes

Ingredients:
1. 1 can (15 oz) butter beans, drained and rinsed
2. 1/2 cup sunflower seeds, roasted and unsalted
3. 2 garlic cloves, minced
4. 3 tablespoons fresh lemon juice
5. 2 tablespoons tahini
6. 1/4 cup extra-virgin olive oil
7. 1/2 teaspoon ground cumin
8. Salt and pepper to taste
9. 2-3 tablespoons water (as needed for desired consistency)
10. Optional: Fresh herbs (like parsley or cilantro) for garnish

Instructions:
1. In a food processor or blender, combine the drained and rinsed butter beans, sunflower seeds, minced garlic, fresh lemon juice, tahini, olive oil, ground cumin, salt, and pepper.
2. Blend the mixture until smooth and creamy. If the mixture is too thick, add water, 1 tablespoon at a time, until you reach your desired consistency.
3. Taste and adjust seasonings if necessary. If you prefer a stronger lemon flavor, you can add more lemon juice.
4. Once the dip reaches the desired consistency and flavor, transfer it to a serving bowl.
5. If using, garnish with fresh herbs like parsley or cilantro.
6. Serve the Butter Bean and Sunflower Seed Dip with your favorite crackers, sliced veggies, or as a spread for sandwiches.

Nutrition Information:
Note: Nutritional values are approximate and may vary based on specific ingredients and portion sizes.
- Calories: 120 per 2-tablespoon serving, Protein: 4g, Fat: 8g, Carbohydrates: 9g, Fiber: 2g, Sugar: 1g, Sodium: 85mg
Enjoy the wholesome flavors and nutritious benefits of this Butter Bean and Sunflower Seed Dip!

30. Butter Bean and Minted Pea Dip

Explore the delightful world of butter beans with this refreshing and nutritious Butter Bean and Minted Pea Dip. Packed with protein, fiber, and vibrant flavors, this dip is a versatile addition to your healthy eating repertoire. The combination of creamy butter beans and sweet peas, enhanced with the invigorating touch of fresh mint, creates a dip that's not only delicious but also an excellent source of nutrients. Perfect for spreading on whole-grain crackers, dipping fresh veggies, or as a side dish for your favorite meals, this recipe makes healthy eating a delightful experience.

Serving: Serve the Butter Bean and Minted Pea Dip in a bowl alongside whole-grain crackers, sliced cucumbers, or carrot sticks for a satisfying and nutritious snack or appetizer.
Preparation Time: 15 minutes
Ready Time: 15 minutes

Ingredients:
- 1 can (15 ounces) butter beans, drained and rinsed
- 1 cup frozen peas, thawed
- 2 tablespoons fresh mint leaves, chopped
- 1 clove garlic, minced
- 2 tablespoons extra-virgin olive oil
- 1 tablespoon lemon juice
- Salt and pepper to taste
- Optional: Greek yogurt for added creaminess

Instructions:

1. In a food processor, combine the butter beans, peas, mint, and minced garlic.
2. Pulse the ingredients until they are roughly chopped and blended.
3. With the food processor running, gradually add the olive oil and lemon juice until the mixture reaches a smooth and creamy consistency.
4. Season the dip with salt and pepper to taste. Adjust the seasonings as needed.
5. If desired, incorporate Greek yogurt for added creaminess, adjusting the quantity based on your preference.
6. Transfer the dip to a serving bowl and garnish with a sprig of mint for a fresh touch.
7. Serve with your favorite dippables, such as whole-grain crackers, sliced vegetables, or pita bread.

Nutrition Information:
Note: Nutrition Information may vary based on specific ingredients used and serving sizes.
- Calories per serving: XXX, Protein: XXX grams, Carbohydrates: XXX grams, Dietary Fiber: XXX grams, Sugars: XXX grams, Fat: XXX grams, Saturated Fat: XXX grams, Cholesterol: XXX milligrams, Sodium: XXX milligrams

Enjoy the wholesome goodness of this Butter Bean and Minted Pea Dip as a nourishing addition to your healthy eating habits!

31. Roasted Tomato and Butter Bean Dip

Indulge in the creamy richness of butter beans and the vibrant flavors of roasted tomatoes with this delightful Roasted Tomato and Butter Bean Dip. This recipe combines the earthy goodness of butter beans with the tangy sweetness of roasted tomatoes, creating a dip that's as wholesome as it is delicious. Perfect for gatherings or as a flavorful addition to your snacking repertoire, this dip is both nutritious and satisfying.

Serving: Makes approximately 2 cups of dip
Preparation time: 10 minutes
Ready time: 35 minutes

Ingredients:
- 2 cups cherry tomatoes, halved

- 1 can (15 oz) butter beans, drained and rinsed
- 3 cloves garlic, minced
- 2 tablespoons olive oil
- 1 tablespoon balsamic vinegar
- 1 teaspoon dried oregano
- Salt and pepper to taste
- Optional: 2 tablespoons chopped fresh basil for garnish

Instructions:
1. Preheat your oven to 400°F (200°C).
2. Place the halved cherry tomatoes on a baking sheet lined with parchment paper. Drizzle with 1 tablespoon of olive oil, minced garlic, balsamic vinegar, dried oregano, salt, and pepper. Toss gently to coat.
3. Roast the tomatoes in the preheated oven for about 25-30 minutes or until they begin to caramelize and turn tender. Remove from the oven and let them cool slightly.
4. In a food processor, combine the roasted tomatoes and the drained butter beans.
5. Add the remaining tablespoon of olive oil and blend until the mixture becomes smooth and creamy. If needed, add a splash of water for desired consistency.
6. Season the dip with additional salt and pepper to taste.
7. Transfer the dip to a serving bowl, garnish with chopped fresh basil if desired, and serve with your favorite dippers like pita chips, veggie sticks, or crackers.

Nutrition Information:
(Per 2-tablespoon serving)
- Calories: 45, Total Fat: 2g, Saturated Fat: 0.3g, Cholesterol: 0mg, Sodium: 65mg
- Total Carbohydrate: 6g, Dietary Fiber: 2g, Sugars: 1g, Protein: 2g

This dip is not only a flavorful addition to your table but also a great source of fiber and protein, making it a healthy choice for any occasion. Enjoy the wholesome goodness of butter beans and roasted tomatoes in each bite!

32. Butter Bean and Charred Corn Hummus

Butter beans, with their creamy texture and nutty flavor, add a delightful twist to traditional hummus. Combined with charred corn, this recipe elevates the classic dip to new heights, offering a healthy and flavorful alternative. Packed with protein and fiber, this butter bean and charred corn hummus is not only delicious but also a nutritious addition to any meal or snack.

Serving: 6 servings
Preparation time: 15 minutes
Ready time: 25 minutes

Ingredients:
- 2 cups cooked butter beans (canned or cooked from dried beans)
- 1 cup charred corn kernels (from about 2 ears of corn)
- 1/4 cup tahini
- 2 garlic cloves, minced
- 1/4 cup fresh lemon juice
- 2 tablespoons olive oil
- 1 teaspoon ground cumin
- 1/2 teaspoon smoked paprika
- Salt and pepper to taste
- 2-4 tablespoons water (as needed for consistency)
- Optional garnishes: drizzle of olive oil, chopped parsley, extra charred corn

Instructions:
1. Char the corn: Heat a skillet or grill pan over medium-high heat. Add the corn and cook, turning occasionally, until charred in spots, about 5-7 minutes. Remove from heat and let it cool. Once cooled, cut the kernels off the cobs and set aside.
2. In a food processor, combine the cooked butter beans, charred corn kernels, tahini, minced garlic, lemon juice, olive oil, ground cumin, smoked paprika, salt, and pepper.
3. Blend the ingredients until smooth, scraping down the sides of the processor as needed. If the mixture is too thick, add water, 1 tablespoon at a time, until desired consistency is reached.
4. Taste and adjust seasoning if necessary, adding more salt, pepper, or lemon juice according to your preference.
5. Transfer the butter bean and charred corn hummus to a serving bowl. If desired, drizzle with olive oil, sprinkle with chopped parsley, and top with extra charred corn for garnish.

6. Serve with fresh vegetables, pita bread, or crackers. Enjoy this flavorful and nutritious dip!

Nutrition Information
(per serving):
- Calories: 180, Total Fat: 9g, Saturated Fat: 1g, Cholesterol: 0mg, Sodium: 150mg
- Total Carbohydrate: 20g, Dietary Fiber: 6g, Sugars: 1g, Protein: 7g
Note: Nutrition Information is approximate and may vary based on specific ingredients used. Adjustments can be made based on dietary needs or preferences.

33. Butter Bean and Herbed Ricotta Dip

This Butter Bean and Herbed Ricotta Dip is a delightful blend of creamy butter beans, tangy ricotta, and fresh herbs. It's a nutritious dip that offers a satisfyingly smooth texture and a burst of flavors. Perfect for gatherings or as a healthy snack, this recipe elevates the versatility of butter beans in a deliciously wholesome way.
 Serving:
- Serves: 6-8 people
- Serving size: 2 tablespoons
 Preparation time:
- Prep: 15 minutes
 Ready time:
- Ready in: 20 minutes

Ingredients:
- 1 can (15 ounces) butter beans, drained and rinsed
- 1 cup ricotta cheese
- 2 cloves garlic, minced
- 2 tablespoons fresh lemon juice
- Zest of 1 lemon
- 2 tablespoons chopped fresh parsley
- 1 tablespoon chopped fresh thyme leaves
- Salt and black pepper to taste
- 2 tablespoons extra-virgin olive oil
- Optional: Red pepper flakes for a hint of spice

- For serving: Fresh vegetables, whole grain crackers, or pita chips

Instructions:
1. Prepare Butter Beans: Rinse and drain the butter beans thoroughly. Set aside.
2. Blend Ingredients: In a food processor, combine the butter beans, ricotta cheese, minced garlic, lemon juice, lemon zest, chopped parsley, and thyme leaves. Blend until the mixture becomes smooth and creamy.
3. Season and Adjust: Season with salt and black pepper according to taste preferences. For a bit of heat, add red pepper flakes if desired. Blend again to incorporate the seasoning evenly.
4. Drizzle with Olive Oil: While the food processor is running, slowly drizzle in the extra-virgin olive oil. This helps in achieving a silky texture and enhances the flavors.
5. Adjust Consistency: If the dip is too thick, add a splash of water or more olive oil, a teaspoon at a time, and blend until the desired consistency is reached.
6. Serve: Transfer the dip to a serving bowl. Garnish with a drizzle of olive oil, fresh herbs, and a sprinkle of red pepper flakes if desired. Serve with an assortment of fresh vegetables, whole grain crackers, or pita chips.

Nutrition Information
(per serving - 2 tablespoons):
- Calories: 110, Total Fat: 7g, Saturated Fat: 2.5g, Trans Fat: 0g, Cholesterol: 15mg, Sodium: 110mg, Total Carbohydrates: 8g, Dietary Fiber: 2g, Sugars: 0g, Protein: 5g
Note: Nutritional values are approximate and may vary based on specific ingredients used.

34. Butter Bean and Green Chile Dip

Indulge in the wholesome goodness of our Butter Bean and Green Chile Dip—a delightful concoction that not only tantalizes your taste buds but also celebrates the nutritious charm of butter beans. This versatile legume takes center stage in this recipe, showcasing its velvety texture and mild, nutty flavor. Paired with the vibrant kick of green chiles, this dip is a stellar addition to your collection of healthy and satisfying recipes.

Serving: 8 servings
Preparation Time: 15 minutes
Ready Time: 30 minutes

Ingredients:
- 2 cans (15 ounces each) butter beans, drained and rinsed
- 1 cup diced green chiles (fresh or canned)
- 1/4 cup extra-virgin olive oil
- 2 cloves garlic, minced
- 1 tablespoon fresh lemon juice
- 1 teaspoon ground cumin
- 1/2 teaspoon smoked paprika
- Salt and pepper to taste
- 2 tablespoons chopped fresh cilantro (optional, for garnish)
- Whole grain pita chips or vegetable sticks for serving

Instructions:
1. In a food processor, combine the butter beans, diced green chiles, olive oil, minced garlic, fresh lemon juice, ground cumin, and smoked paprika.
2. Pulse the ingredients until the mixture reaches a smooth and creamy consistency. If needed, scrape down the sides of the food processor and pulse again to ensure even blending.
3. Season the dip with salt and pepper to taste, adjusting the flavors according to your preference.
4. Transfer the dip to a serving bowl and garnish with chopped fresh cilantro, if desired.
5. Serve the Butter Bean and Green Chile Dip with whole grain pita chips or a colorful array of vegetable sticks for a wholesome and satisfying snack or appetizer.

Nutrition Information:
Per serving (1/8th of the recipe):
- Calories: 160, Total Fat: 8g, Saturated Fat: 1g, Cholesterol: 0mg, Sodium: 290mg, Total Carbohydrates: 18g, Dietary Fiber: 4g, Sugars: 2g, Protein: 5g

Note: Nutrition Information is approximate and may vary based on specific ingredients used. Adjust serving sizes and ingredient quantities accordingly.

35. Butter Bean and Lemon Zest Hummus

Discover a delightful twist to traditional hummus with our Butter Bean and Lemon Zest Hummus recipe. Packed with the goodness of butter beans and a zesty kick from fresh lemon zest, this healthy alternative is a perfect addition to your repertoire of nutritious snacks. The creamy texture of butter beans combined with the citrusy brightness of lemon creates a unique and irresistible flavor profile. Dive into a world of wholesome indulgence with this Butter Bean and Lemon Zest Hummus—where health meets indulgence.

Serving: Makes approximately 2 cups of hummus.
Preparation Time: 15 minutes
Ready Time: 15 minutes

Ingredients:
- 1 can (15 ounces) butter beans, drained and rinsed
- 2 cloves garlic, minced
- 3 tablespoons tahini
- 1/4 cup fresh lemon juice
- 1 teaspoon lemon zest
- 1/2 teaspoon ground cumin
- 1/4 cup extra-virgin olive oil
- Salt and pepper, to taste
- Water (as needed for desired consistency)

Instructions:
1. In a food processor, combine the butter beans, minced garlic, tahini, fresh lemon juice, lemon zest, and ground cumin.
2. Pulse the ingredients until well combined.
3. With the food processor running, slowly drizzle in the extra-virgin olive oil until the hummus reaches a smooth and creamy consistency.
4. Season with salt and pepper to taste. If the hummus is too thick, add water, one tablespoon at a time, until it reaches your desired consistency.

5. Continue to blend until all ingredients are well incorporated and the hummus is velvety smooth.
6. Taste and adjust the seasoning if necessary.
7. Transfer the Butter Bean and Lemon Zest Hummus to a serving bowl.
8. Drizzle with a bit of olive oil and sprinkle with additional lemon zest for garnish.
9. Serve with fresh vegetable sticks, pita bread, or your favorite whole-grain crackers.

Nutrition Information:
(Per 2-tablespoon serving)
- Calories: 80, Total Fat: 6g, Saturated Fat: 1g, Cholesterol: 0mg, Sodium: 80mg, Total Carbohydrates: 5g, Dietary Fiber: 1g, Sugars: 0g, Protein: 2g
Indulge in this guilt-free treat that not only satisfies your taste buds but also nourishes your body with the wholesome goodness of butter beans and the refreshing zest of lemon.

36. Butter Bean and Horseradish Dip

Elevate your snack game with this wholesome and flavorful Butter Bean and Horseradish Dip. Packed with protein and fiber from butter beans, and a zesty kick from horseradish, this dip is not only delicious but also a nutritious addition to your table. Perfect for parties, gatherings, or a simple afternoon snack, it's a versatile and easy-to-make recipe that showcases the versatility of butter beans in creating healthy and satisfying dishes.

Serving: Makes about 2 cups of dip, serving 6-8 people.
Preparation Time: 15 minutes
Ready Time: 1 hour (including chilling time)

Ingredients:
- 2 cans (15 ounces each) butter beans, drained and rinsed
- 1/4 cup plain Greek yogurt
- 2 tablespoons olive oil
- 2 tablespoons fresh lemon juice
- 2 cloves garlic, minced
- 1 tablespoon horseradish (adjust to taste)

- 1 teaspoon ground cumin
- Salt and pepper to taste
- Fresh parsley, chopped, for garnish

Instructions:
1. In a food processor, combine the butter beans, Greek yogurt, olive oil, lemon juice, minced garlic, horseradish, and ground cumin.
2. Blend until smooth and creamy, scraping down the sides as needed to ensure all ingredients are well incorporated.
3. Season with salt and pepper to taste, adjusting the horseradish if more heat is desired.
4. Transfer the dip to a serving bowl, cover, and refrigerate for at least 1 hour to allow the flavors to meld.
5. Before serving, garnish with fresh chopped parsley for a burst of color and freshness.
6. Serve with an array of crisp, colorful vegetables, whole-grain crackers, or pita bread.

Nutrition Information:
(Per Serving - based on 1/8th of the recipe)
- Calories: ~120, Protein: ~5g, Carbohydrates: ~15g, Fiber: ~4g, Fat: ~5g, Saturated Fat: ~1g, Cholesterol: ~1mg, Sodium: ~180mg
Note: Nutrition Information may vary based on specific ingredients and serving sizes. Adjust quantities accordingly for individual dietary preferences.

37. Butter Bean and Cranberry Dip

Indulge in the wholesome goodness of our Butter Bean and Cranberry Dip—a delightful creation that combines the earthy richness of butter beans with the sweet-tart burst of cranberries. This healthy dip is not only a flavorful addition to your snack repertoire but also a celebration of the versatile butter bean, packed with nutrients and fiber. Perfect for gatherings or a solo treat, this dip effortlessly marries health and indulgence.

Serving: Makes approximately 2 cups of dip
Preparation Time: 15 minutes

Ready Time: 15 minutes

Ingredients:
- 1 can (15 ounces) butter beans, drained and rinsed
- 1/2 cup dried cranberries
- 2 cloves garlic, minced
- 2 tablespoons tahini
- 3 tablespoons extra-virgin olive oil
- 2 tablespoons lemon juice
- 1 teaspoon ground cumin
- 1/2 teaspoon paprika
- Salt and pepper to taste
- Water (as needed for consistency)
- Fresh parsley for garnish (optional)

Instructions:
1. In a food processor, combine the butter beans, dried cranberries, minced garlic, tahini, olive oil, lemon juice, ground cumin, paprika, salt, and pepper.
2. Blend the ingredients until smooth, pausing to scrape down the sides as needed. If the mixture is too thick, add water, one tablespoon at a time, until you achieve your desired consistency.
3. Taste the dip and adjust the seasonings if necessary, adding more salt, pepper, or lemon juice to suit your preferences.
4. Transfer the dip to a serving bowl, drizzle with a bit of olive oil, and garnish with fresh parsley if desired.
5. Serve with an array of dippables such as whole-grain pita chips, vegetable sticks, or whole-wheat crackers.

Nutrition Information:
(Per 2 tablespoons)
- Calories: 70, Total Fat: 4g, Saturated Fat: 0.5g, Cholesterol: 0mg, Sodium: 80mg, Total Carbohydrates: 8g, Dietary Fiber: 2g, Sugars: 3g, Protein: 2g

Enjoy the vibrant flavors and nutritional benefits of this Butter Bean and Cranberry Dip—your go-to guilt-free snack!

38. Roasted Red Cabbage and Butter Bean Hummus

Elevate your culinary experience with this nutritious and flavorful recipe for Roasted Red Cabbage and Butter Bean Hummus. Packed with the goodness of butter beans and the vibrant hues of roasted red cabbage, this hummus is not only a feast for the eyes but also a powerhouse of nutrients. The creamy texture and rich flavors make it a perfect addition to your repertoire of healthy, delicious recipes.

Serving: 4 servings
Preparation Time: 15 minutes
Ready Time: 45 minutes

Ingredients:
- 1 cup butter beans, cooked and drained
- 2 cups red cabbage, thinly sliced
- 3 tablespoons olive oil, divided
- 1 garlic clove, minced
- 2 tablespoons tahini
- Juice of 1 lemon
- 1 teaspoon ground cumin
- Salt and pepper to taste
- 1 tablespoon fresh parsley, chopped (for garnish)

Instructions:
1. Preheat the Oven:
Preheat your oven to 400°F (200°C).
2. Roast the Red Cabbage:
Place the thinly sliced red cabbage on a baking sheet. Drizzle with 2 tablespoons of olive oil and season with salt and pepper. Toss to coat evenly. Roast in the preheated oven for 20-25 minutes or until the cabbage edges are crisp and slightly browned. Remove from the oven and let it cool.
3. Prepare the Butter Beans:
In a food processor, combine the cooked and drained butter beans, roasted red cabbage, minced garlic, tahini, lemon juice, ground cumin, and 1 tablespoon of olive oil. Blend until smooth and creamy. If needed, add a splash of water to achieve your desired consistency.
4. Season to Perfection:

Taste the hummus and adjust the seasoning with salt and pepper according to your preference. Blend once more to incorporate the seasonings.

5. Serve:

Transfer the Roasted Red Cabbage and Butter Bean Hummus to a serving dish. Drizzle with a bit of olive oil and garnish with chopped fresh parsley.

6. Enjoy:

Serve with your favorite fresh veggies, pita bread, or whole-grain crackers. Enjoy the wholesome goodness of this unique and nutritious hummus!

Nutrition Information

(per serving):
- Calories: 180, Protein: 6g, Fat: 10g, Carbohydrates: 20g, Fiber: 5g, Sugar: 2g, Sodium: 220mg

This Roasted Red Cabbage and Butter Bean Hummus is a delightful twist on traditional hummus, providing a colorful and nutrient-packed addition to your healthy eating journey.

39. Butter Bean and Goat Cheese Dip

Indulge in the wholesome goodness of butter beans with our delectable Butter Bean and Goat Cheese Dip. This nutrient-packed dip is not only a flavorful treat for your taste buds but also a fantastic way to incorporate the health benefits of butter beans into your diet. Creamy goat cheese adds a luxurious touch, making this dip a perfect companion for your favorite veggies or whole-grain crackers.

Serving: 6-8 servings

Preparation time: 15 minutes

Ready time: 30 minutes

Ingredients:
- 2 cans (15 ounces each) butter beans, drained and rinsed
- 4 ounces goat cheese, crumbled
- 1/4 cup extra-virgin olive oil
- 2 cloves garlic, minced
- 1 tablespoon lemon juice

- 1 teaspoon ground cumin
- 1/2 teaspoon paprika
- Salt and pepper to taste
- Fresh parsley, chopped, for garnish (optional)

Instructions:
1. In a food processor, combine the butter beans, goat cheese, olive oil, minced garlic, lemon juice, ground cumin, paprika, salt, and pepper.
2. Blend the ingredients until smooth and creamy, scraping down the sides of the food processor as needed.
3. Taste the dip and adjust the seasonings if necessary.
4. Transfer the dip to a serving bowl, and if desired, garnish with chopped fresh parsley for a burst of color and freshness.
5. Serve the Butter Bean and Goat Cheese Dip with an assortment of sliced vegetables, such as carrots, cucumbers, and bell peppers, or with whole-grain crackers.

Nutrition Information:
Note: Nutrition values are approximate and may vary based on specific ingredients and serving sizes.
- Calories: 150 per serving, Total Fat: 10g, Saturated Fat: 4g, Trans Fat: 0g, Cholesterol: 10mg, Sodium: 200mg, Total Carbohydrates: 12g, Dietary Fiber: 4g, Sugars: 1g, Protein: 6g

Dive into the goodness of this Butter Bean and Goat Cheese Dip – a delightful and nutritious addition to your healthy eating repertoire. Enjoy the rich flavors and creamy texture while knowing you're fueling your body with wholesome ingredients.

40. Butter Bean and Caper Tapenade

Butter beans, with their creamy texture and nutty flavor, are a versatile legume that can be transformed into a variety of nutritious dishes. This Butter Bean and Caper Tapenade is a delightful spread bursting with Mediterranean flavors, perfect for spreading on toast, crackers, or as a dip for veggies. Packed with protein, fiber, and essential nutrients, this recipe showcases the versatility and health benefits of butter beans in a deliciously tangy and savory tapenade.

Serving: Makes approximately 1 ½ cups of tapenade.
Preparation Time: 15 minutes
Ready Time: 15 minutes

Ingredients:
- 1 can (15 ounces) butter beans, drained and rinsed
- 1/4 cup capers, drained
- 2 cloves garlic, minced
- 1/4 cup fresh parsley, chopped
- 2 tablespoons lemon juice
- 3 tablespoons extra-virgin olive oil
- Salt and pepper to taste

Instructions:
1. Prepare the Beans: Rinse and drain the butter beans thoroughly. Pat them dry using a clean kitchen towel or paper towels to remove excess moisture.
2. Blend Ingredients: In a food processor, combine the butter beans, capers, minced garlic, chopped parsley, and lemon juice.
3. Blend and Drizzle Olive Oil: Pulse the ingredients together while slowly drizzling in the olive oil. Continue pulsing until the mixture becomes a coarse paste. You can adjust the consistency by adding more olive oil if desired.
4. Season to Taste: Taste the tapenade and season with salt and pepper according to your preference. Pulse a few more times to incorporate the seasoning evenly.
5. Serve or Store: Transfer the tapenade to a bowl and serve immediately as a spread on toast, crackers, or as a dip for fresh vegetables. Alternatively, store it in an airtight container in the refrigerator for up to one week.

Nutrition Information
(per 2 tablespoons):
- Calories: 60, Total Fat: 4g, Saturated Fat: 0.5g, Cholesterol: 0mg, Sodium: 230mg
- Total Carbohydrate: 5g, Dietary Fiber: 1g, Sugars: 0g, Protein: 2g

This Butter Bean and Caper Tapenade is a quick and simple recipe that brings out the best of butter beans, offering a healthy and flavorful addition to any meal or snack.

41. Butter Bean and Miso Dip

This Butter Bean and Miso Dip offers a delightful fusion of flavors that elevate the humble butter bean to new heights. Creamy and rich, with a hint of umami from the miso, this dip is not only delicious but also packed with nutrients. It's a fantastic addition to any spread, perfect for dipping veggies, crackers, or spreading on sandwiches.

Serving:
- Serves: 6-8 people
- Serving suggestion: Enjoy as a dip with fresh vegetable sticks, whole-grain crackers, or as a spread for sandwiches or wraps.

Preparation Time:
- Prep Time: 10 minutes

Ready Time:
- Ready In: 15 minutes

Ingredients:
- 2 cans (15 oz each) butter beans, drained and rinsed
- 2 tablespoons white miso paste
- 2 cloves garlic, minced
- 2 tablespoons olive oil
- Juice of 1 lemon
- 2 tablespoons tahini
- 1/4 teaspoon smoked paprika (optional)
- Salt and pepper to taste
- Water (as needed for consistency)
- Optional garnishes: chopped fresh herbs (parsley, chives), drizzle of olive oil

Instructions:
1. Prepare the Butter Beans: Rinse and drain the butter beans thoroughly.
2. Blend Ingredients: In a food processor or blender, combine the butter beans, white miso paste, minced garlic, olive oil, lemon juice, tahini, and smoked paprika if using.
3. Blend Until Smooth: Pulse or blend the mixture until smooth. If the mixture is too thick, add water a tablespoon at a time until desired consistency is reached.

4. Season to Taste: Taste the dip and season with salt and pepper as needed. Adjust lemon juice or other seasonings to suit your preference.
5. Serve: Transfer the dip to a serving bowl. Optionally, drizzle with olive oil and garnish with chopped fresh herbs.
6. Enjoy: Serve with your choice of accompaniments like fresh veggies, crackers, or use as a spread for sandwiches.

Nutrition Information:
- Per Serving (1/8th of the recipe):
- Calories: 130, Total Fat: 6g, Saturated Fat: 1g, Sodium: 290mg
- Total Carbohydrate: 15g, Dietary Fiber: 4g, Sugars: 1g, Protein: 5g
- Vitamin D: 0%
- Calcium: 4%
- Iron: 10%
- Potassium: 6%

Feel free to adjust the seasonings and ingredients according to your taste preferences. This nutritious dip is a versatile addition to any meal or snack time!

42. Butter Bean and Tzatziki Hummus

In the realm of healthy and versatile ingredients, butter beans reign supreme. Their creamy texture and mild flavor make them an excellent canvas for diverse culinary creations. This Butter Bean and Tzatziki Hummus recipe embodies both nutrition and flavor, blending the earthiness of butter beans with the freshness of tzatziki for a delightful twist on traditional hummus.

Serving: 6 servings
Preparation Time: 10 minutes
Ready Time: 15 minutes

Ingredients:
- 2 cups cooked butter beans (canned, drained, and rinsed)
- 1/2 cup Greek yogurt
- 1/4 cup tahini
- 2 cloves garlic, minced
- 2 tablespoons extra-virgin olive oil

- 2 tablespoons fresh lemon juice
- 1 teaspoon ground cumin
- 1/2 teaspoon paprika
- Salt and pepper to taste
- 1/2 cucumber, grated and squeezed to remove excess moisture
- 1 tablespoon chopped fresh dill
- Optional: Additional olive oil and paprika for garnish

Instructions:
1. In a food processor, combine the cooked butter beans, Greek yogurt, tahini, minced garlic, olive oil, lemon juice, ground cumin, paprika, salt, and pepper.
2. Blend the mixture until smooth and creamy, scraping down the sides of the processor as needed to ensure all ingredients are well combined.
3. In a separate bowl, mix the grated cucumber and chopped fresh dill. If desired, season lightly with salt and pepper.
4. Fold the cucumber-dill mixture into the butter bean hummus, gently incorporating it to add texture and a hint of freshness.
5. Taste and adjust seasoning as necessary, adding more salt, pepper, or lemon juice according to your preference.
6. Transfer the hummus to a serving dish, drizzle with a touch of olive oil, and sprinkle with paprika for an appealing finish.
7. Serve the Butter Bean and Tzatziki Hummus with vegetable sticks, whole-grain pita bread, or as a spread for sandwiches or wraps.

Nutrition Information
(per serving):
- Calories: 180, Total Fat: 10g, Saturated Fat: 1.5g, Cholesterol: 1mg, Sodium: 230mg, Total Carbohydrates: 16g, Dietary Fiber: 4g, Sugars: 1.5g, Protein: 8g
Note: Nutritional values are approximate and may vary based on specific ingredients used.

43. Butter Bean and Honey Mustard Dip

Discover the delightful combination of wholesome butter beans and the tangy kick of honey mustard in this nutritious Butter Bean and Honey Mustard Dip. Packed with protein, fiber, and flavor, this versatile dip is not only delicious but also a fantastic addition to your healthy eating repertoire. Perfect for gatherings, snacks, or as a spread, this recipe is a celebration of simplicity and nutrition.

Serving: Ideal for 4-6 people.
Preparation Time: 15 minutes
Ready Time: 20 minutes

Ingredients:
- 2 cups cooked butter beans (canned or freshly cooked)
- 3 tablespoons honey mustard
- 2 tablespoons extra-virgin olive oil
- 1 clove garlic, minced
- 1 tablespoon fresh lemon juice
- Salt and pepper to taste
- Optional: Chopped fresh herbs (such as parsley or chives) for garnish

Instructions:
1. Prepare Butter Beans: If using canned butter beans, drain and rinse them under cold water. If using freshly cooked butter beans, ensure they are cooled to room temperature.
2. Blend Ingredients: In a food processor, combine the butter beans, honey mustard, olive oil, minced garlic, and fresh lemon juice. Blend until smooth and creamy.
3. Season to Taste: Taste the dip and season with salt and pepper according to your preference. Blend again to incorporate the seasoning.
4. Garnish (Optional): If desired, add a sprinkle of chopped fresh herbs like parsley or chives to enhance the flavor and visual appeal of the dip.
5. Serve: Transfer the Butter Bean and Honey Mustard Dip to a serving bowl. Serve with an array of colorful vegetable sticks, whole grain crackers, or pita wedges.
6. Enjoy: Dive into the wholesome goodness of this dip and savor the unique combination of butter beans and honey mustard.

Nutrition Information:
Note: Nutrition Information is approximate and may vary based on specific ingredients used.
- Calories: 150 per serving, Protein: 6g, Carbohydrates: 20g, Dietary Fiber: 5g, Fat: 7g, Saturated Fat: 1g, Cholesterol: 0mg, Sodium: 200mg

Embrace a healthier snacking option with this Butter Bean and Honey Mustard Dip, where flavor meets nutrition in every creamy bite.

44. Creamy Butter Bean and Sage Dip

Elevate your snack game with this delightful and nutritious Creamy Butter Bean and Sage Dip. Butter beans, also known as lima beans, take center stage in this recipe, providing a creamy texture and a wealth of health benefits. Paired with the earthy aroma of sage, this dip is a perfect balance of flavors that will satisfy your taste buds while keeping things light and wholesome.

Serving: Makes approximately 2 cups of dip.
Preparation Time: 15 minutes
Ready Time: 15 minutes

Ingredients:
- 2 cans (15 ounces each) butter beans, drained and rinsed
- 2 cloves garlic, minced
- 2 tablespoons fresh lemon juice
- 1/4 cup extra-virgin olive oil
- 1 tablespoon fresh sage, finely chopped
- Salt and black pepper to taste
- Optional garnish: a drizzle of olive oil and fresh sage leaves

Instructions:
1. In a food processor, combine the butter beans, minced garlic, fresh lemon juice, and olive oil.
2. Blend the mixture until smooth and creamy. If needed, scrape down the sides of the food processor to ensure all ingredients are well incorporated.
3. Add the finely chopped sage to the creamy bean mixture. Pulse the food processor a few times to incorporate the sage evenly into the dip.
4. Taste the dip and season with salt and black pepper to your liking. Adjust the flavors as needed.
5. Transfer the creamy butter bean and sage dip to a serving bowl.
6. If desired, garnish the dip with a drizzle of olive oil and a few fresh sage leaves.

7. Serve the dip with an assortment of fresh vegetables, whole-grain crackers, or pita bread.

Nutrition Information:
Note: Nutrition Information is approximate and may vary based on specific ingredients used and portion sizes.
- Serving Size: 1/4 cup
- Calories: 80, Total Fat: 4.5g, Saturated Fat: 0.5g, Trans Fat: 0g, Cholesterol: 0mg, Sodium: 120mg, Total Carbohydrates: 8g, Dietary Fiber: 2g, Sugars: 0g, Protein: 3g
Note:
Feel free to customize this Creamy Butter Bean and Sage Dip by adjusting the seasonings or incorporating your favorite herbs. This versatile dip can be a healthy addition to your snacking routine or a flavorful appetizer for gatherings.

45. Roasted Red Kale and Butter Bean Hummus

Roasted Red Kale and Butter Bean Hummus is a nutritious twist on traditional hummus, incorporating the goodness of butter beans and the earthy flavor of roasted kale. Packed with protein, fiber, and vitamins, this vibrant hummus offers a delicious way to enjoy a healthy snack or a flavorful spread.
 Serving:
Serves: 4-6
 Preparation time:
Prep: 15 minutes
 Ready time:
Total: 35 minutes

Ingredients:
- 1 can (15 oz) butter beans, drained and rinsed
- 2 cups red kale, stems removed and chopped
- 2 garlic cloves, minced
- 3 tablespoons tahini
- 2 tablespoons lemon juice
- 2 tablespoons olive oil
- 1 teaspoon cumin

- 1/2 teaspoon paprika
- Salt and pepper to taste

Instructions:
1. Preheat Oven: Preheat your oven to 375°F (190°C).
2. Roast Kale: On a baking sheet, spread out the chopped red kale. Drizzle with a tablespoon of olive oil, sprinkle with salt and pepper, then toss to coat. Roast in the preheated oven for 10-12 minutes or until the kale becomes crispy. Remove and let it cool.
3. Prepare Butter Beans: In a food processor, combine the drained butter beans, roasted kale, minced garlic, tahini, lemon juice, cumin, paprika, and the remaining olive oil. Blend until smooth and creamy, scraping down the sides as needed. If the consistency is too thick, add a splash of water to achieve your desired texture.
4. Season to Taste: Taste the hummus and adjust the seasoning with salt, pepper, or additional lemon juice according to your preference.
5. Serve: Transfer the roasted red kale and butter bean hummus to a serving bowl. Drizzle with a touch of olive oil and sprinkle with a pinch of paprika for garnish, if desired.

Nutrition Information
(per serving):
- Calories: 180, Total Fat: 10g, Saturated Fat: 1.5g, Cholesterol: 0mg, Sodium: 210mg
- Total Carbohydrate: 18g, Dietary Fiber: 5g
- Total Sugars: 1g, Protein: 7g

Enjoy this Roasted Red Kale and Butter Bean Hummus with your favorite veggies, pita bread, or as a spread on sandwiches for a wholesome and flavorful treat!

46. Butter Bean and Pomegranate Dip

Indulge in the vibrant and nutritious world of butter beans with our delectable Butter Bean and Pomegranate Dip. This recipe seamlessly blends the velvety texture of butter beans with the burst of sweetness from pomegranate seeds, creating a wholesome dip that not only tantalizes your taste buds but also packs a nutritional punch. Perfect for gatherings or as a delightful snack, this dip celebrates the versatility and health benefits of butter beans in a delightful culinary creation.

Serving: Makes approximately 2 cups of dip.
Preparation Time: 15 minutes
Ready Time: 15 minutes

Ingredients:
- 1 can (15 ounces) butter beans, drained and rinsed
- 1/2 cup pomegranate seeds
- 2 tablespoons tahini
- 2 tablespoons extra-virgin olive oil
- 1 clove garlic, minced
- 1 tablespoon fresh lemon juice
- 1/2 teaspoon ground cumin
- Salt and pepper to taste
- Fresh parsley, chopped, for garnish
- Pomegranate arils for additional garnish (optional)

Instructions:
1. Prepare the Butter Beans:
- Rinse and drain the canned butter beans thoroughly.
2. Blend
Ingredients:
- In a food processor, combine the butter beans, pomegranate seeds, tahini, olive oil, minced garlic, fresh lemon juice, ground cumin, salt, and pepper.
3. Blend Until Smooth:
- Process the ingredients until the mixture is smooth and well combined. If needed, scrape down the sides of the food processor to ensure all ingredients are incorporated.
4. Adjust Seasoning:
- Taste the dip and adjust the salt, pepper, or lemon juice according to your preference.
5. Serve:
- Transfer the dip to a serving bowl. Drizzle with a bit of olive oil and sprinkle fresh parsley and additional pomegranate arils on top for a burst of color and flavor.
6. Garnish:

- Garnish with additional pomegranate arils and fresh parsley for a visually appealing presentation.
7. Serve and Enjoy:
- Serve the Butter Bean and Pomegranate Dip with your favorite whole-grain crackers, vegetable sticks, or pita bread. Enjoy this nutritious and flavorful dip with friends and family.

Nutrition Information:
Note: Nutrition Information is approximate and may vary based on specific ingredients used.
- Calories: 120 per 1/4 cup serving, Protein: 4g, Fat: 7g, Carbohydrates: 12g, Fiber: 3g, Sugar: 2g, Sodium: 150mg
Embrace the goodness of butter beans with this delightful dip that not only satisfies your cravings but also promotes a healthy and balanced lifestyle.

47. Butter Bean and Gorgonzola Dip

Explore the rich and creamy world of Butter Bean and Gorgonzola Dip—a delectable blend of wholesome butter beans and the bold flavor of Gorgonzola cheese. This nutritious dip is not only a delightful party appetizer but also a versatile addition to your healthy eating repertoire. Packed with protein and fiber, this recipe showcases the versatility of butter beans, offering a guilt-free indulgence that will leave your taste buds dancing. Let's dive into the simple steps to create this irresistibly creamy and flavorful dip.

Serving: Makes approximately 2 cups of dip.
Preparation Time: 15 minutes
Ready Time: 20 minutes

Ingredients:
- 1 can (15 ounces) butter beans, drained and rinsed
- 1/2 cup crumbled Gorgonzola cheese
- 1/4 cup plain Greek yogurt
- 2 tablespoons olive oil
- 1 clove garlic, minced
- 1 tablespoon lemon juice

- Salt and pepper to taste
- Optional: Chopped fresh herbs (such as parsley or chives) for garnish

Instructions:
1. Prepare the Butter Beans:
- Rinse and drain the butter beans thoroughly. This helps remove excess sodium and ensures a smoother consistency for the dip.
2. Combine

Ingredients:
- In a food processor, combine the butter beans, Gorgonzola cheese, Greek yogurt, olive oil, minced garlic, and lemon juice.
3. Blend Until Smooth:
- Process the ingredients until you achieve a smooth and creamy consistency. Stop occasionally to scrape down the sides of the food processor, ensuring an even blend.
4. Season to Taste:
- Add salt and pepper to taste, adjusting the seasoning as needed. The Gorgonzola provides a bold flavor, so be mindful of the salt quantity.
5. Garnish (Optional):
- If desired, sprinkle chopped fresh herbs, such as parsley or chives, on top for a burst of color and added freshness.
6. Serve:
- Transfer the dip to a serving bowl and pair it with an array of colorful vegetable sticks, whole-grain crackers, or pita wedges.
7.

Nutrition Information:
- Note: Nutrition Information is approximate and may vary based on specific ingredients and serving sizes.
- Calories: 120 per 1/4 cup serving, Protein: 6g, Fat: 8g, Carbohydrates: 8g, Fiber: 2g, Sugar: 1g, Sodium: 180mg

Enjoy this Butter Bean and Gorgonzola Dip as a guilt-free snack or a crowd-pleasing party appetizer. Its rich flavors and nutritional benefits make it a perfect addition to your healthy eating routine.

48. Butter Bean and Green Onion Hummus

This Butter Bean and Green Onion Hummus is a delightful twist on the classic chickpea-based dip. Packed with protein and fiber from butter beans, this hummus offers a unique and satisfying flavor profile enhanced by the freshness of green onions. Perfect for snacking, spreading on sandwiches, or as a vibrant party dip, this recipe is a nutritious and delicious addition to your repertoire of healthy recipes.

Serving: Makes approximately 2 cups of hummus
Preparation Time: 15 minutes
Ready Time: 15 minutes

Ingredients:
- 2 cups cooked butter beans (canned or freshly cooked)
- 3 green onions, chopped
- 2 cloves garlic, minced
- 1/4 cup tahini
- 1/4 cup extra-virgin olive oil
- Juice of 1 lemon
- 1 teaspoon ground cumin
- Salt and pepper, to taste
- Water (as needed for desired consistency)
- Optional toppings: chopped green onions, a drizzle of olive oil, paprika

Instructions:
1. Prepare Butter Beans: If using canned butter beans, drain and rinse them thoroughly. If cooking from scratch, ensure they are fully cooked and cooled.
2. Combine Ingredients: In a food processor, combine the butter beans, chopped green onions, minced garlic, tahini, olive oil, lemon juice, ground cumin, salt, and pepper.
3. Blend: Process the ingredients until smooth, stopping to scrape down the sides of the food processor as needed. If the mixture is too thick, add water gradually until you achieve your desired consistency.
4. Taste and Adjust: Taste the hummus and adjust the seasoning if necessary. Add more salt, pepper, or lemon juice according to your preference.
5. Serve: Transfer the hummus to a serving bowl. If desired, garnish with additional chopped green onions, a drizzle of olive oil, and a sprinkle of paprika.

6. Enjoy: Serve with your favorite fresh vegetables, pita bread, or whole-grain crackers.

Nutrition Information:
Note: Nutritional values are approximate and may vary based on specific ingredients and serving sizes.
- Calories per serving: 150, Total Fat: 10g, Saturated Fat: 1.5g, Trans Fat: 0g, Cholesterol: 0mg, Sodium: 180mg, Total Carbohydrates: 12g, Dietary Fiber: 3g, Sugars: 1g, Protein: 5g

This Butter Bean and Green Onion Hummus not only satisfies your taste buds but also provides a nutritious alternative to traditional hummus. Enjoy the creamy texture and unique flavor that butter beans and green onions bring to this healthy and versatile dip.

49. Butter Bean and Cucumber Dip

Embrace the wholesome goodness of butter beans with this refreshing and nutritious Butter Bean and Cucumber Dip. Packed with protein and fiber, this dip not only satisfies your taste buds but also contributes to a healthy lifestyle. The combination of creamy butter beans and crisp cucumbers creates a delightful texture, while the blend of herbs and spices adds a burst of flavor. Serve this dip with whole-grain crackers or fresh vegetable sticks for a guilt-free snack that's as delicious as it is nourishing.

Serving: Makes approximately 2 cups of dip.
Preparation Time: 15 minutes
Ready Time: 15 minutes

Ingredients:
- 1 can (15 oz) butter beans, drained and rinsed
- 1 cucumber, peeled, seeded, and diced
- 2 cloves garlic, minced
- 2 tablespoons fresh lemon juice
- 2 tablespoons extra-virgin olive oil
- 1 tablespoon tahini
- 1 teaspoon ground cumin
- 1/2 teaspoon paprika

- Salt and pepper to taste
- 2 tablespoons fresh parsley, chopped (for garnish)

Instructions:
1. In a food processor, combine the butter beans, diced cucumber, minced garlic, fresh lemon juice, olive oil, tahini, ground cumin, paprika, salt, and pepper.
2. Blend the ingredients until smooth and creamy. If the mixture is too thick, you can add a little water, one tablespoon at a time, until you reach your desired consistency.
3. Taste the dip and adjust the seasonings if necessary. Add more salt, pepper, or lemon juice to suit your preferences.
4. Transfer the dip to a serving bowl and refrigerate for at least 30 minutes to allow the flavors to meld.
5. Before serving, garnish with chopped fresh parsley for a pop of color and added freshness.

Nutrition Information:
Note: Nutrition Information is approximate and may vary based on specific ingredients used.
- Serving Size: 1/4 cup
- Calories: 80, Total Fat: 5g, Saturated Fat: 0.7g, Trans Fat: 0g, Cholesterol: 0mg, Sodium: 120mg, Total Carbohydrates: 7g, Dietary Fiber: 2g, Sugars: 1g, Protein: 3g

Enjoy this Butter Bean and Cucumber Dip as a wholesome snack or a delightful addition to your party platter. It's a tasty and nutritious way to incorporate butter beans into your diet!

50. Butter Bean and Roasted Eggplant Hummus

Elevate your healthy eating journey with this delightful Butter Bean and Roasted Eggplant Hummus recipe. Packed with protein-rich butter beans and the smoky goodness of roasted eggplant, this hummus is a flavorful twist on the classic dip. Perfect for parties, snacks, or spreading on your favorite whole-grain crackers or vegetables, this recipe not only satisfies your taste buds but also nourishes your body with essential nutrients.

Serving: Makes approximately 2 cups of hummus.
Preparation Time: 15 minutes
Ready Time: 45 minutes (including roasting time)

Ingredients:
- 1 can (15 ounces) butter beans, drained and rinsed
- 1 medium-sized eggplant, roasted and peeled
- 3 tablespoons tahini
- 2 cloves garlic, minced
- 2 tablespoons extra-virgin olive oil, plus extra for drizzling
- Juice of 1 lemon
- 1 teaspoon ground cumin
- 1/2 teaspoon smoked paprika
- Salt and pepper, to taste
- Fresh parsley, for garnish (optional)
- Red pepper flakes, for a spicy kick (optional)

Instructions:
1. Roast the Eggplant:
- Preheat the oven to 400°F (200°C).
- Pierce the eggplant several times with a fork and place it on a baking sheet.
- Roast for 30-40 minutes or until the skin is charred and the inside is soft.
- Let the eggplant cool, then peel away the charred skin.
2. Prepare the Hummus:
- In a food processor, combine the drained butter beans, roasted and peeled eggplant, tahini, minced garlic, olive oil, lemon juice, cumin, smoked paprika, salt, and pepper.
- Blend until smooth and creamy. If the mixture is too thick, add a bit of water or extra olive oil until you reach your desired consistency.
3. Adjust Seasoning:
- Taste the hummus and adjust the seasoning as needed. You can add more salt, pepper, or lemon juice to suit your preferences.
4. Serve:
- Transfer the hummus to a serving bowl. Drizzle with extra olive oil and garnish with fresh parsley and red pepper flakes if desired.

Nutrition Information:
- Serving Size: 2 tablespoons

- Calories: 80, Total Fat: 5g, Saturated Fat: 1g, Cholesterol: 0mg, Sodium: 120mg, Total Carbohydrates: 7g, Dietary Fiber: 2g, Sugars: 1g, Protein: 2.5g

Enjoy this wholesome Butter Bean and Roasted Eggplant Hummus as a nutritious dip or spread, and feel good about treating yourself to a snack that's as good for your taste buds as it is for your body.

51. Butter Bean and Lemon Pepper Dip

Embrace the wholesome goodness of butter beans with our delectable Butter Bean and Lemon Pepper Dip. This nutrient-packed dip is not only a savory delight but also a fantastic addition to your healthy eating journey. Butter beans, known for their creamy texture and mild flavor, take center stage in this recipe, perfectly complemented by the zesty kick of lemon pepper. Whether you're entertaining guests or looking for a guilt-free snack, this dip is a delicious way to savor the nutritious benefits of butter beans.

Serving: Makes approximately 2 cups of dip.
Preparation Time: 15 minutes
Ready Time: 15 minutes

Ingredients:
- 2 cups cooked butter beans (canned or freshly cooked)
- 2 tablespoons olive oil
- 1 clove garlic, minced
- 2 tablespoons fresh lemon juice
- 1 teaspoon lemon zest
- 1 teaspoon lemon pepper seasoning
- 1/2 teaspoon salt (adjust to taste)
- 1/4 teaspoon black pepper
- 2 tablespoons fresh parsley, chopped (for garnish)

Instructions:
1. Prepare the Butter Beans:
- If using canned butter beans, drain and rinse them thoroughly. If using fresh beans, cook them according to package instructions until tender.
2. Blend the

Ingredients:
- In a food processor, combine the cooked butter beans, olive oil, minced garlic, fresh lemon juice, lemon zest, lemon pepper seasoning, salt, and black pepper.

3. Blend Until Smooth:
- Process the ingredients until the mixture is smooth and creamy. If needed, scrape down the sides of the food processor and blend again for a consistent texture.

4. Adjust Seasoning:
- Taste the dip and adjust the seasoning if necessary. Add more salt, pepper, or lemon juice to suit your preferences.

5. Serve:
- Transfer the dip to a serving bowl. Drizzle with a bit of olive oil and sprinkle chopped fresh parsley on top for a burst of color and added flavor.

6. Garnish and Enjoy:
- Garnish with additional lemon zest or parsley if desired. Serve the Butter Bean and Lemon Pepper Dip with your favorite vegetable sticks, whole-grain crackers, or pita bread.

Nutrition Information:
Note: Nutritional values are approximate and may vary based on specific ingredients used.
- Calories: 120 per 1/4 cup serving, Protein: 5g, Fat: 5g, Carbohydrates: 15g, Fiber: 4g, Sugar: 1g

Delight in the wholesome flavors and health benefits of our Butter Bean and Lemon Pepper Dip—an excellent addition to your collection of nutritious and delicious recipes.

52. Roasted Garlic and Butter Bean Hummus

Roasted Garlic and Butter Bean Hummus is a creamy, nutrient-rich twist on traditional hummus. Packed with the goodness of butter beans and the deep, earthy flavor of roasted garlic, this dip is a wholesome and versatile addition to any meal or snack. Enjoy it as a spread, a dip for veggies, or a flavorful topping for sandwiches and wraps.

Serving: Makes about 2 cups of hummus
Preparation time: 10 minutes

Ready time: 45 minutes

Ingredients:
- 2 cups cooked butter beans (canned or soaked and boiled)
- 1 head of garlic
- 2 tablespoons olive oil
- 2 tablespoons tahini
- Juice of 1 lemon
- 2 tablespoons water (or more for desired consistency)
- 1/2 teaspoon cumin powder
- Salt and pepper to taste
- Optional: Paprika and fresh parsley for garnish

Instructions:
1. Roast the Garlic: Preheat your oven to 400°F (200°C). Cut the top off the head of garlic to expose the cloves. Place the head of garlic on a piece of foil, drizzle with a bit of olive oil, wrap it in the foil, and roast in the oven for 30-35 minutes until the cloves are soft and golden. Let it cool.
2. Prepare the Hummus: In a food processor, combine the cooked butter beans, tahini, lemon juice, cumin powder, salt, and pepper.
3. Add Roasted Garlic: Squeeze the roasted garlic cloves from their skins and add them to the food processor.
4. Blend: Pulse the mixture while drizzling in the olive oil. Gradually add water until you reach your desired creamy consistency. Scrape down the sides as needed and blend until smooth.
5. Adjust Seasoning: Taste and adjust the seasoning, adding more salt, pepper, or lemon juice as desired.
6. Serve: Transfer the hummus to a bowl. If preferred, drizzle a bit of olive oil over the top, sprinkle with paprika, and garnish with fresh parsley.

Nutrition Information
(per 2 tablespoon serving):
- Calories: 60, Total Fat: 3.5g, Saturated Fat: 0.5g, Sodium: 80mg, Total Carbohydrates: 5g, Dietary Fiber: 1.5g, Sugars: 0.5g, Protein: 2g
Nutritional values are approximate and may vary based on specific ingredients used.

53. Butter Bean and Za'atar Dip

This butter bean and za'atar dip is a deliciously wholesome addition to any table. Butter beans, with their creamy texture, blend perfectly with the aromatic flavors of za'atar, creating a dip that's both nutritious and bursting with Middle Eastern zest. Enjoy it as a snack with veggie sticks or as a spread on toast for a delightful and healthy treat.

Serving: 8 servings
Preparation time: 10 minutes
Ready time: 15 minutes

Ingredients:
- 2 cups cooked butter beans
- 2 tablespoons olive oil
- 2 tablespoons tahini
- 2 cloves garlic, minced
- 1 tablespoon za'atar spice blend
- Juice of 1 lemon
- Salt to taste
- Optional: 2 tablespoons chopped fresh parsley for garnish

Instructions:
1. Prepare the Butter Beans: Rinse and drain the cooked butter beans thoroughly. If using canned beans, ensure they are well-rinsed.
2. Blend Ingredients: In a food processor, combine the butter beans, olive oil, tahini, minced garlic, za'atar spice blend, lemon juice, and a pinch of salt.
3. Blend Until Smooth: Pulse the mixture until it reaches a smooth and creamy consistency. If needed, scrape down the sides of the processor and blend again to ensure all ingredients are well incorporated.
4. Adjust Seasoning: Taste the dip and adjust the seasoning by adding more salt or lemon juice if desired.
5. Serve: Transfer the dip to a serving bowl. If preferred, drizzle a little extra olive oil on top and sprinkle with chopped fresh parsley for added flavor and presentation.

Nutrition Information
(per serving):
- Calories: 120, Total Fat: 7g, Saturated Fat: 1g, Trans Fat: 0g, Cholesterol: 0mg, Sodium: 135mg

- Total Carbohydrate: 11g, Dietary Fiber: 3g, Sugars: 1g, Protein: 4g
Note: Nutritional values are approximate and may vary based on specific ingredients used.
This delightful butter bean and za'atar dip is a nutritious and versatile option for a healthy snack or appetizer, packed with protein, fiber, and fantastic flavors that will tantalize your taste buds.

54. Butter Bean and Harissa Hummus

Elevate your snacking experience with this nutritious and flavorful Butter Bean and Harissa Hummus. Butter beans, also known as lima beans, add a creamy texture and a boost of protein to this classic Middle Eastern dip. The addition of harissa, a North African chili paste, gives it a spicy kick that will tantalize your taste buds. This wholesome hummus is not only delicious but also a healthy way to enjoy the versatility of butter beans. Spread it on whole-grain crackers, use it as a dip for fresh veggies, or slather it on your favorite sandwich for a satisfying and nutrient-packed treat.

Serving: 8 servings
Preparation time: 15 minutes
Ready time: 20 minutes

Ingredients:
- 2 cups cooked butter beans (canned or freshly cooked)
- 3 tablespoons tahini
- 2 tablespoons olive oil
- 2 tablespoons harissa paste (adjust to taste)
- 2 cloves garlic, minced
- 1 teaspoon ground cumin
- Juice of 1 lemon
- Salt to taste
- Water (as needed for desired consistency)
- Fresh parsley, chopped (for garnish)

Instructions:
1. Rinse and drain the cooked butter beans if using canned beans.
2. In a food processor, combine the butter beans, tahini, olive oil, harissa paste, minced garlic, ground cumin, and lemon juice.

3. Blend the ingredients until smooth, scraping down the sides as needed. If the mixture is too thick, add water gradually until you achieve your desired consistency.
4. Taste the hummus and add salt as needed. Adjust the harissa paste to your preferred level of spiciness.
5. Continue blending until the hummus is creamy and well combined.
6. Transfer the hummus to a serving dish, drizzle with a bit of olive oil, and garnish with chopped fresh parsley.
7. Serve with whole-grain crackers, pita bread, or an assortment of fresh vegetables.

Nutrition Information
(per serving):
- Calories: 160, Protein: 7g, Fat: 9g, Carbohydrates: 16g, Fiber: 4g, Sugar: 1g, Sodium: 200mg

Enjoy this Butter Bean and Harissa Hummus as a wholesome and satisfying snack or appetizer that packs a punch of flavor and nutrition.

55. Butter Bean and Mango Salsa

Elevate your culinary experience with this vibrant and nutritious Butter Bean and Mango Salsa—a delightful fusion of wholesome butter beans and the tropical sweetness of mango. Bursting with flavors and packed with essential nutrients, this recipe not only tantalizes your taste buds but also adds a touch of health to your plate. Perfect as a side dish or a standalone snack, this salsa embodies the essence of a healthy and delicious culinary journey.

Serving: 4 servings
Preparation time: 15 minutes
Ready time: 20 minutes

Ingredients:
- 1 can (15 oz) butter beans, drained and rinsed
- 1 ripe mango, diced
- 1/2 red onion, finely chopped
- 1 red bell pepper, diced
- 1 jalapeño, seeds removed and finely chopped
- 1/4 cup fresh cilantro, chopped

- Juice of 2 limes
- 2 tablespoons extra-virgin olive oil
- Salt and pepper, to taste
- Tortilla chips, for serving (optional)

Instructions:
1. In a large bowl, combine the butter beans, diced mango, red onion, red bell pepper, jalapeño, and cilantro.
2. In a small bowl, whisk together the lime juice and extra-virgin olive oil. Pour the dressing over the bean and mango mixture.
3. Gently toss the ingredients until well combined, ensuring the dressing evenly coats the beans and mango.
4. Season with salt and pepper to taste. Adjust the seasoning as needed.
5. Allow the salsa to marinate for at least 5 minutes to let the flavors meld.
6. Serve the Butter Bean and Mango Salsa in a bowl, accompanied by tortilla chips if desired.

Nutrition Information:
Per Serving (approximate values)
- Calories: 180 kcal, Total Fat: 7g, Saturated Fat: 1g, Trans Fat: 0g, Cholesterol: 0mg, Sodium: 180mg, Total Carbohydrates: 28g, Dietary Fiber: 6g, Sugars: 10g, Protein: 4g

Indulge in the goodness of this Butter Bean and Mango Salsa—a dish that not only satisfies your taste buds but also contributes to your overall well-being. Enjoy the perfect balance of textures and flavors in every spoonful, and make it a staple in your healthy eating repertoire.

56. Butter Bean and Roasted Tomato Salsa

This vibrant Butter Bean and Roasted Tomato Salsa is a delightful addition to your collection of healthy recipes. Packed with the goodness of butter beans and the robust flavors of roasted tomatoes, this salsa is a versatile and nutritious accompaniment that can elevate any dish. Whether served as a refreshing dip, a side dish, or a topping for grilled proteins, it's a flavorful way to incorporate the wholesome benefits of butter beans into your diet.

Serving: Makes approximately 2 cups of salsa.
Preparation Time: 15 minutes
Ready Time: 40 minutes

Ingredients:
- 1 can (15 ounces) butter beans, drained and rinsed
- 1 pint cherry tomatoes, halved
- 1 small red onion, finely diced
- 2 cloves garlic, minced
- 2 tablespoons olive oil
- 1 teaspoon balsamic vinegar
- 1 teaspoon honey
- Salt and pepper to taste
- 1/4 cup fresh basil, chopped

Instructions:
1. Preheat the oven: Preheat your oven to 400°F (200°C).
2. Roast the tomatoes: Place the halved cherry tomatoes on a baking sheet. Drizzle with 1 tablespoon of olive oil and season with salt and pepper. Roast in the preheated oven for 25-30 minutes or until the tomatoes are caramelized and slightly wrinkled.
3. Prepare the butter beans: While the tomatoes are roasting, in a medium bowl, combine the drained butter beans, diced red onion, and minced garlic.
4. Make the dressing: In a small bowl, whisk together the remaining 1 tablespoon of olive oil, balsamic vinegar, and honey.
5. Combine and toss: Once the tomatoes are roasted, let them cool slightly. Add the roasted tomatoes to the bowl with butter beans, red onion, and garlic. Pour the dressing over the mixture and gently toss until well combined.
6. Finish with basil: Fold in the fresh chopped basil, adjusting salt and pepper to taste.
7. Chill (optional): For enhanced flavors, cover the salsa and refrigerate for at least 15 minutes before serving.
8. Serve: Enjoy the Butter Bean and Roasted Tomato Salsa as a side dish, dip, or topping for grilled proteins.

Nutrition Information:
Note: Nutrition values are approximate and may vary based on specific ingredients used.

- Calories: 120 per 1/2 cup serving, Protein: 4g, Carbohydrates: 18g, Dietary Fiber: 4g, Sugars: 5g, Fat: 5g, Saturated Fat: 1g, Cholesterol: 0mg, Sodium: 180mg

57. Butter Bean and Pine Nut Dip

Discover a delightful and nutritious way to enjoy the wholesome goodness of butter beans with our Butter Bean and Pine Nut Dip. This versatile dip is not only a treat for your taste buds but also a powerhouse of nutrients. Packed with protein, fiber, and healthy fats, it's a perfect addition to your collection of healthy recipes. The creamy texture of butter beans combines harmoniously with the rich flavor of pine nuts, creating a dip that's as satisfying as it is good for you.

Serving: Ideal for sharing, this recipe serves 4-6 people as a delightful appetizer or snack.
Preparation Time: 15 minutes
Ready Time: 15 minutes

Ingredients:
- 1 can (15 oz) butter beans, drained and rinsed
- 1/4 cup pine nuts, lightly toasted
- 2 cloves garlic, minced
- 2 tablespoons fresh lemon juice
- 3 tablespoons extra-virgin olive oil
- 1 tablespoon tahini
- 1/2 teaspoon ground cumin
- Salt and pepper to taste
- Fresh parsley for garnish (optional)

Instructions:
1. In a food processor, combine the drained and rinsed butter beans, toasted pine nuts, minced garlic, fresh lemon juice, olive oil, tahini, ground cumin, salt, and pepper.
2. Blend the ingredients until smooth and creamy, scraping down the sides of the processor as needed to ensure everything is well combined.
3. Taste the dip and adjust the seasonings to your preference, adding more salt, pepper, or lemon juice as needed.

4. Once the dip reaches your desired consistency and flavor, transfer it to a serving bowl.
5. If desired, garnish with a sprinkle of fresh parsley for a burst of color and added freshness.
6. Serve the Butter Bean and Pine Nut Dip with your favorite vegetable sticks, whole-grain crackers, or pita wedges.

Nutrition Information:
(Per serving - based on 6 servings)
- Calories: 180, Protein: 5g, Fat: 14g, Saturated Fat: 2g, Carbohydrates: 10g, Fiber: 3g, Sugar: 1g, Sodium: 200mg
Enjoy this flavorful and nutritious Butter Bean and Pine Nut Dip as a wholesome snack or appetizer that celebrates the goodness of butter beans in a delicious and healthy way.

58. Butter Bean and Roasted Carrot Hummus

Elevate your snack game with this nutritious and flavorful Butter Bean and Roasted Carrot Hummus. Packed with protein, fiber, and essential nutrients, this twist on traditional hummus is a delightful way to enjoy the goodness of butter beans. The addition of roasted carrots not only enhances the vibrant color but also introduces a subtle sweetness that perfectly complements the earthy flavor of butter beans. Get ready to dip into a wholesome and delicious spread that's as good for your taste buds as it is for your well-being.

Serving: Makes approximately 2 cups of hummus.
Preparation Time: 15 minutes
Ready Time: 45 minutes

Ingredients:
- 1 can (15 ounces) butter beans, drained and rinsed
- 2 medium carrots, peeled and cut into small chunks
- 3 tablespoons olive oil, divided
- 2 cloves garlic, minced
- 3 tablespoons tahini
- Juice of 1 lemon
- 1 teaspoon ground cumin

- 1/2 teaspoon smoked paprika
- Salt and pepper to taste
- Water (as needed for consistency)
- Optional garnish: chopped fresh parsley, drizzle of olive oil

Instructions:
1. Roast the Carrots: Preheat the oven to 400°F (200°C). Toss the carrot chunks with 1 tablespoon of olive oil and spread them on a baking sheet. Roast for 20-25 minutes or until the carrots are tender and slightly caramelized. Allow them to cool.
2. Prepare the Hummus Base: In a food processor, combine the butter beans, roasted carrots, minced garlic, tahini, lemon juice, cumin, smoked paprika, salt, and pepper.
3. Blend until Smooth: While the food processor is running, drizzle in the remaining 2 tablespoons of olive oil and blend until the hummus reaches a smooth consistency. If needed, add water gradually to achieve the desired thickness.
4. Adjust Seasoning: Taste the hummus and adjust the seasoning according to your preference. Add more salt, pepper, or lemon juice if necessary.
5. Serve: Transfer the hummus to a serving dish. Garnish with chopped fresh parsley and a drizzle of olive oil for an extra touch of freshness.
6. Enjoy: Serve the Butter Bean and Roasted Carrot Hummus with your favorite vegetables, pita bread, or whole-grain crackers. It's a delicious and nutritious snack or appetizer.

Nutrition Information:
Note: Nutritional values are approximate and may vary based on specific ingredients and serving sizes.
- Calories: 120 per 1/4 cup serving, Protein: 4g, Fat: 8g, Carbohydrates: 10g, Fiber: 3g, Sugar: 1g, Sodium: 180mg

59. Butter Bean and Kimchi Dip

Elevate your snack game with this delectable Butter Bean and Kimchi Dip! Packed with the wholesome goodness of butter beans and the bold flavors of kimchi, this dip is not only delicious but also a nutritious addition to your repertoire of healthy recipes. The creamy texture of butter beans combined with the tangy and spicy kick from kimchi creates a flavor profile that will leave your taste buds wanting more. Perfect for gatherings, parties, or just a cozy night in, this dip is a versatile crowd-pleaser.

Serving: Ideal for 6-8 people as an appetizer or snack.
Preparation Time: 15 minutes
Ready Time: 15 minutes

Ingredients:
- 2 cups canned butter beans, drained and rinsed
- 1 cup kimchi, chopped
- 1/4 cup Greek yogurt
- 2 tablespoons tahini
- 2 tablespoons olive oil
- 1 clove garlic, minced
- 1 teaspoon soy sauce
- 1 teaspoon rice vinegar
- 1/2 teaspoon sesame oil
- Salt and pepper to taste
- Optional toppings: chopped green onions, sesame seeds

Instructions:
1. In a food processor, combine the drained and rinsed butter beans, chopped kimchi, Greek yogurt, tahini, olive oil, minced garlic, soy sauce, rice vinegar, and sesame oil.
2. Blend the ingredients until smooth, scraping down the sides of the processor as needed.
3. Taste the dip and adjust the seasoning with salt and pepper as desired.
4. Transfer the dip to a serving bowl and garnish with chopped green onions and sesame seeds if desired.
5. Serve immediately with an assortment of fresh vegetables, whole grain crackers, or pita chips.

Nutrition Information:
Note: Nutrition Information is approximate and may vary based on specific ingredients and serving sizes.
- Serving Size: 1/4 cup

- Calories: 120, Total Fat: 8g, Saturated Fat: 1g, Trans Fat: 0g, Cholesterol: 0mg, Sodium: 180mg, Total Carbohydrates: 10g, Dietary Fiber: 3g, Sugars: 1g, Protein: 4g

Tip: Feel free to customize the dip to your taste by adjusting the amount of kimchi for more or less spice. Experiment with different dippers like carrot sticks, cucumber slices, or whole grain tortilla chips for a wholesome and satisfying snack.

60. Butter Bean and Jalapeño Hummus

Transform your humble butter beans into a zesty and nutritious delight with this Butter Bean and Jalapeño Hummus recipe. Packed with protein, fiber, and a kick of spice, this healthy twist on traditional hummus is perfect for snacking or as a flavorful spread. Embrace the goodness of butter beans in a whole new way!

Serving: 8 servings
Preparation Time: 10 minutes
Ready Time: 15 minutes

Ingredients:
- 2 cups cooked butter beans (canned or boiled)
- 1/4 cup tahini
- 1/4 cup extra-virgin olive oil
- 2 tablespoons fresh lemon juice
- 2 cloves garlic, minced
- 1 teaspoon ground cumin
- 1/2 teaspoon smoked paprika
- 1/2 teaspoon salt (adjust to taste)
- 1/4 cup pickled jalapeños, drained (adjust for preferred spice level)
- 2 tablespoons chopped fresh cilantro (optional, for garnish)

Instructions:
1. Prepare the Butter Beans:
- If using canned butter beans, drain and rinse them thoroughly. If using dried beans, cook them according to package instructions until they are soft and can be easily mashed.
2. Blend
Ingredients:

- In a food processor, combine the cooked butter beans, tahini, olive oil, lemon juice, minced garlic, ground cumin, smoked paprika, and salt. Blend until smooth and creamy.

3. Add Jalapeños:
- Add the pickled jalapeños to the mixture. Blend again until the jalapeños are evenly incorporated, giving the hummus a delightful spicy kick.

4. Adjust Consistency:
- If the hummus is too thick, add a bit of water or extra olive oil, one tablespoon at a time, until you reach your desired consistency.

5. Taste and Adjust:
- Taste the hummus and adjust the seasoning, adding more salt or lemon juice if needed.

6. Serve:
- Transfer the hummus to a serving bowl. Drizzle with a bit of olive oil and sprinkle chopped cilantro on top for an extra burst of freshness.

7. Enjoy:
- Serve the Butter Bean and Jalapeño Hummus with pita bread, vegetable sticks, or your favorite whole-grain crackers.

Nutrition Information
(per serving):
- Calories: 180, Protein: 6g, Fat: 12g, Carbohydrates: 16g, Fiber: 4g, Sugar: 1g, Sodium: 250mg

Elevate your snack game with this Butter Bean and Jalapeño Hummus—a delicious and nutritious twist on a classic favorite. It's the perfect embodiment of the health benefits and versatility of butter beans.

61. Butter Bean and Cumin Dip

Elevate your snacking experience with this wholesome Butter Bean and Cumin Dip—a delightful addition to our collection of "Healthy Ways to Use Butter Beans Recipes." Packed with protein, fiber, and a burst of flavor from cumin, this dip is both nutritious and satisfying. Perfect for gatherings or a solo indulgence, it's a versatile dish that embodies the goodness of butter beans in a mouthwatering blend.

Serving: Makes approximately 2 cups of dip.

Preparation Time: 15 minutes
Ready Time: 15 minutes

Ingredients:
- 2 cans (15 ounces each) butter beans, drained and rinsed
- 3 tablespoons olive oil
- 2 tablespoons fresh lemon juice
- 2 cloves garlic, minced
- 1 teaspoon ground cumin
- 1/2 teaspoon paprika
- Salt and pepper to taste
- Fresh parsley for garnish (optional)

Instructions:
1. In a food processor, combine the drained and rinsed butter beans, olive oil, fresh lemon juice, minced garlic, ground cumin, paprika, salt, and pepper.
2. Blend the ingredients until smooth and creamy. If the dip is too thick, you can add a bit more olive oil or a splash of water to reach your desired consistency.
3. Taste the dip and adjust the seasoning according to your preference. Add more salt, pepper, or lemon juice as needed.
4. Once the dip is well-blended and seasoned, transfer it to a serving bowl.
5. Garnish with fresh parsley if desired, and drizzle a bit of olive oil on top for an extra touch of richness.
6. Serve the Butter Bean and Cumin Dip with your favorite vegetable sticks, pita chips, or whole-grain crackers.

Nutrition Information:
Per serving (2 tablespoons):
- Calories: 80, Total Fat: 4.5g, Saturated Fat: 0.5g, Cholesterol: 0mg, Sodium: 120mg, Total Carbohydrates: 8g, Dietary Fiber: 2g, Sugars: 0g, Protein: 2g
Note: Nutrition Information is approximate and may vary based on specific ingredients and serving sizes.

62. Butter Bean and Tomato Basil Dip

Indulge in the wholesome goodness of butter beans with this delectable Butter Bean and Tomato Basil Dip. Packed with protein, fiber, and an array of nutrients, this dip is not only delicious but also a nutritious addition to your snack repertoire. The combination of creamy butter beans, vibrant tomatoes, and fragrant basil creates a dip that is perfect for spreading on whole grain crackers, dipping veggies, or even as a sandwich spread. Elevate your snacking experience with this easy-to-make and health-conscious recipe.

Serving: Makes approximately 2 cups of dip.
Preparation Time: 15 minutes
Ready Time: 15 minutes

Ingredients:
- 1 can (15 ounces) butter beans, drained and rinsed
- 1 cup cherry tomatoes, halved
- 2 cloves garlic, minced
- 1/4 cup fresh basil leaves, chopped
- 2 tablespoons extra-virgin olive oil
- 1 tablespoon lemon juice
- Salt and pepper to taste

Instructions:
1. In a food processor, combine the butter beans, cherry tomatoes, minced garlic, and chopped basil.
2. Pulse the ingredients until coarsely blended, scraping down the sides as needed.
3. While the food processor is running, slowly drizzle in the olive oil and lemon juice until the dip reaches a smooth and creamy consistency.
4. Taste the dip and season with salt and pepper as desired. Blend again to incorporate the seasoning.
5. Transfer the Butter Bean and Tomato Basil Dip to a serving bowl.
6. Serve immediately with whole grain crackers, sliced veggies, or use as a spread for sandwiches.

Nutrition Information:
Per 2-tablespoon serving:

- Calories: 60, Total Fat: 3.5g, Saturated Fat: 0.5g, Trans Fat: 0g, Cholesterol: 0mg, Sodium: 120mg, Total Carbohydrates: 6g, Dietary Fiber: 2g, Sugars: 1g, Protein: 2g
Note: Nutrition Information is approximate and may vary based on specific ingredients used.

63. Butter Bean and Pickled Radish Salsa

Elevate your culinary experience with this refreshing Butter Bean and Pickled Radish Salsa—a delightful twist on traditional salsa recipes. Packed with the wholesome goodness of butter beans and the zesty crunch of pickled radishes, this salsa not only tantalizes your taste buds but also adds a nutritious punch to your meals. Versatile and easy to prepare, it's the perfect accompaniment to grilled proteins, tacos, or as a vibrant topping for your favorite salads. Embrace a healthier lifestyle with this vibrant and flavorful Butter Bean and Pickled Radish Salsa.

Serving: 4 servings
Preparation Time: 15 minutes
Ready Time: 15 minutes

Ingredients:
- 1 can (15 oz) butter beans, drained and rinsed
- 1 cup pickled radishes, thinly sliced
- 1/2 red onion, finely diced
- 1/2 cup cherry tomatoes, quartered
- 1/4 cup fresh cilantro, chopped
- 1 jalapeño, finely chopped (seeds removed for milder salsa)
- 1 clove garlic, minced
- 2 tablespoons extra-virgin olive oil
- 1 tablespoon red wine vinegar
- Salt and pepper to taste

Instructions:
1. In a large mixing bowl, combine the butter beans, pickled radishes, diced red onion, quartered cherry tomatoes, chopped cilantro, jalapeño, and minced garlic.

2. In a small bowl, whisk together the extra-virgin olive oil and red wine vinegar. Pour the dressing over the bean and radish mixture.
3. Gently toss the ingredients until well combined, ensuring the dressing evenly coats the salsa.
4. Season with salt and pepper to taste. Adjust the seasoning as needed.
5. Allow the salsa to marinate for at least 10 minutes to let the flavors meld together.
6. Serve the Butter Bean and Pickled Radish Salsa as a side dish, a topping for grilled proteins, or as a vibrant addition to salads and tacos.

Nutrition Information:
(Per serving)
- Calories: 180, Total Fat: 8g, Saturated Fat: 1g, Cholesterol: 0mg, Sodium: 300mg, Total Carbohydrates: 22g, Dietary Fiber: 6g, Sugars: 3g, Protein: 6g
Note: Nutrition Information is approximate and may vary based on specific ingredients used.

64. Butter Bean and Avocado Hummus

Elevate your healthy eating with this nutritious and delicious Butter Bean and Avocado Hummus. Packed with protein, fiber, and heart-healthy fats, this innovative twist on traditional hummus is a delightful way to incorporate butter beans into your diet. The smooth creaminess of butter beans combined with the rich flavor of avocado creates a delectable dip that's perfect for snacking or spreading on your favorite whole-grain crackers or veggies.

Serving: Makes approximately 2 cups of Butter Bean and Avocado Hummus.
Preparation Time: 15 minutes
Ready Time: 15 minutes

Ingredients:
- 1 can (15 ounces) butter beans, drained and rinsed
- 1 ripe avocado, peeled and pitted
- 2 tablespoons tahini
- 3 tablespoons extra-virgin olive oil

- 2 cloves garlic, minced
- Juice of 1 lemon
- 1/2 teaspoon cumin
- Salt and pepper to taste
- Optional garnishes: drizzle of olive oil, paprika, chopped fresh parsley

Instructions:
1. In a food processor, combine the butter beans, avocado, tahini, olive oil, minced garlic, lemon juice, cumin, salt, and pepper.
2. Blend the ingredients until smooth and creamy, scraping down the sides of the food processor as needed.
3. Taste and adjust the seasoning, adding more salt, pepper, or lemon juice if desired.
4. Transfer the hummus to a serving bowl.
5. Optional: Drizzle with olive oil, sprinkle with a pinch of paprika, and garnish with chopped fresh parsley for a vibrant finish.
6. Serve the Butter Bean and Avocado Hummus with your favorite whole-grain crackers, pita bread, or fresh vegetable sticks.

Nutrition Information:
Note: Nutrition Information is approximate and may vary based on specific ingredients used.
- Serving Size: 2 tablespoons
- Calories: 80, Total Fat: 6g, Saturated Fat: 1g, Trans Fat: 0g, Cholesterol: 0mg, Sodium: 80mg, Total Carbohydrates: 5g, Dietary Fiber: 2g, Sugars: 0g, Protein: 2g

This Butter Bean and Avocado Hummus not only satisfies your taste buds but also provides a nutrient-packed boost to support your overall well-being. Enjoy this guilt-free, flavorful dip as a wholesome snack or appetizer.

65. Butter Bean and Roasted Red Pepper Salsa

Explore the delightful world of healthy and flavorful recipes with our "Butter Bean and Roasted Red Pepper Salsa." Packed with nutritious butter beans and the smoky sweetness of roasted red peppers, this vibrant salsa is a versatile addition to your culinary repertoire. Whether you're looking for a refreshing dip, a hearty salad topping, or a wholesome side dish, this recipe has you covered.

Serving: Makes approximately 2 cups of salsa.
Preparation Time: 15 minutes
Ready Time: 30 minutes

Ingredients:
- 1 can (15 ounces) butter beans, drained and rinsed
- 1 cup roasted red peppers, diced (homemade or store-bought)
- 1/2 cup red onion, finely chopped
- 1/4 cup fresh cilantro, chopped
- 2 tablespoons extra-virgin olive oil
- 1 tablespoon red wine vinegar
- 1 clove garlic, minced
- Salt and pepper to taste

Instructions:
1. Prepare the Butter Beans: Drain and rinse the canned butter beans under cold water. Set aside.
2. Roast the Red Peppers: If using fresh red peppers, roast them until the skin is charred. Peel, seed, and dice the roasted red peppers. If using store-bought roasted red peppers, simply dice them.
3. Chop and Combine: In a mixing bowl, combine the butter beans, diced roasted red peppers, chopped red onion, and fresh cilantro.
4. Make the Dressing: In a small bowl, whisk together the extra-virgin olive oil, red wine vinegar, minced garlic, salt, and pepper. Adjust the seasoning according to your taste.
5. Combine and Toss: Pour the dressing over the bean and pepper mixture. Gently toss the ingredients until well combined, ensuring the salsa is evenly coated with the dressing.
6. Chill and Marinate: Cover the bowl and refrigerate for at least 15 minutes to allow the flavors to meld and intensify.
7. Serve: Once chilled, give the salsa a final stir and serve it as a dip with whole-grain chips, as a topping for salads, or as a side dish alongside grilled proteins.

Nutrition Information:
Note: Nutritional values are approximate and may vary based on specific ingredients used.

- Serving Size: 1/2 cup
- Calories: 120, Total Fat: 7g, Saturated Fat: 1g, Cholesterol: 0mg, Sodium: 180mg, Total Carbohydrates: 12g, Dietary Fiber: 3g, Sugars: 2g, Protein: 3g

Embrace the wholesome goodness of butter beans with this Butter Bean and Roasted Red Pepper Salsa – a perfect embodiment of flavor and nutrition. Enjoy the vibrant, healthful journey this recipe brings to your table!

66. Butter Bean and Cilantro Pesto

Explore the delightful world of healthy eating with this Butter Bean and Cilantro Pesto recipe. Butter beans, also known as lima beans, add a creamy texture and a boost of nutrition to this vibrant pesto. Combined with the freshness of cilantro and the richness of nuts, this dish not only satisfies your taste buds but also provides a nutritious punch. Embrace the versatility of butter beans in this unique and flavorful recipe that makes a perfect addition to your collection of wholesome meals.

Serving: 4 servings
Preparation Time: 15 minutes
Ready Time: 20 minutes

Ingredients:
- 2 cups cooked butter beans (canned or soaked and cooked)
- 1 cup fresh cilantro leaves, packed
- 1/2 cup grated Parmesan cheese
- 1/3 cup walnuts or pine nuts
- 2 cloves garlic, minced
- 1/2 cup extra-virgin olive oil
- Juice of 1 lemon
- Salt and pepper to taste

Instructions:
1. In a food processor, combine the cooked butter beans, cilantro, Parmesan cheese, nuts, and minced garlic.
2. Pulse the ingredients until they are coarsely chopped and well combined.

3. With the food processor running, slowly drizzle in the olive oil until the pesto reaches your desired consistency.
4. Add the lemon juice and season with salt and pepper to taste. Blend until all the ingredients are fully incorporated.
5. Taste the pesto and adjust the seasoning or add more olive oil if needed.

Nutrition Information:
Note: Nutritional values are approximate and may vary based on specific ingredients used.
- Calories: 320 per serving, Protein: 10g, Fat: 25g, Carbohydrates: 15g, Fiber: 5g, Sugar: 1g

Pair this Butter Bean and Cilantro Pesto with whole-grain pasta, spread it on toast, or use it as a dip for fresh vegetables. It's a delicious and nutritious way to enjoy the health benefits of butter beans in your daily meals.

67. Butter Bean and Green Olive Tapenade

Elevate your culinary experience with this vibrant and nutritious Butter Bean and Green Olive Tapenade. Bursting with flavors, this recipe combines the creamy texture of butter beans with the briny kick of green olives, creating a delightful spread that's perfect for a variety of dishes. Whether you're spreading it on whole-grain crackers, using it as a dip for fresh veggies, or incorporating it into your favorite wraps, this tapenade offers a healthy twist to your meals.

Serving: Makes approximately 1.5 cups of tapenade.
Preparation Time: 15 minutes
Ready Time: 15 minutes

Ingredients:
- 1 can (15 ounces) butter beans, drained and rinsed
- 1 cup green olives, pitted
- 2 cloves garlic, minced
- 2 tablespoons fresh lemon juice
- 2 tablespoons extra-virgin olive oil
- 1 teaspoon Dijon mustard

- 1 teaspoon capers
- 1/2 teaspoon dried oregano
- Salt and pepper to taste
- Optional: Red pepper flakes for a hint of spice

Instructions:
1. In a food processor, combine the butter beans, green olives, minced garlic, lemon juice, olive oil, Dijon mustard, capers, and dried oregano.
2. Pulse the ingredients until a coarse paste forms, scraping down the sides as needed.
3. Season with salt and pepper to taste. If you prefer a bit of heat, add red pepper flakes to your liking.
4. Continue to pulse until the tapenade reaches your desired consistency – smooth or slightly chunky.
5. Taste and adjust the seasonings as needed.
6. Transfer the tapenade to a bowl and refrigerate for at least 15 minutes to allow the flavors to meld.
7. Serve as a dip with fresh vegetables, spread on whole-grain crackers, or use it as a flavorful addition to wraps and sandwiches.

Nutrition Information:
(Per 2 tablespoons)
- Calories: 70, Total Fat: 5g, Saturated Fat: 0.5g, Cholesterol: 0mg, Sodium: 250mg, Total Carbohydrates: 5g, Dietary Fiber: 2g, Sugars: 0g, Protein: 2g

This Butter Bean and Green Olive Tapenade is not only a delicious addition to your meals but also a wholesome source of plant-based protein and heart-healthy fats. Enjoy the goodness of butter beans in a new and exciting way!

68. Butter Bean and Smoked Almond Dip

Elevate your snack game with this delightful Butter Bean and Smoked Almond Dip—a nutritious twist on the classic dip. Butter beans, known for their creamy texture and mild flavor, take center stage in this recipe, while the addition of smoked almonds brings a rich, smoky depth. Packed with protein and fiber, this dip not only satisfies your taste buds but also nourishes your body. It's a versatile and healthy option for parties, gatherings, or even a simple afternoon snack.

Serving: This recipe yields approximately 2 cups of Butter Bean and Smoked Almond Dip, serving 8 people as an appetizer.
Preparation Time: 15 minutes
Ready Time: 15 minutes

Ingredients:
- 1 can (15 ounces) butter beans, drained and rinsed
- 1/2 cup smoked almonds
- 2 cloves garlic, minced
- 2 tablespoons fresh lemon juice
- 1/4 cup extra-virgin olive oil
- 1 teaspoon smoked paprika
- Salt and pepper to taste
- 2 tablespoons fresh parsley, chopped (for garnish)

Instructions:
1. In a food processor, combine the butter beans, smoked almonds, minced garlic, and fresh lemon juice.
2. Pulse the ingredients until coarsely chopped.
3. With the food processor running, slowly pour in the olive oil until the mixture becomes smooth and creamy.
4. Add smoked paprika, salt, and pepper to taste. Continue blending until all ingredients are well incorporated.
5. Taste the dip and adjust seasoning if necessary.
6. Transfer the dip to a serving bowl and garnish with chopped fresh parsley.
7. Serve immediately with an assortment of fresh vegetables, whole-grain crackers, or pita bread.

Nutrition Information:
Per Serving (1/4 cup):
- Calories: 120, Total Fat: 9g, Saturated Fat: 1g, Trans Fat: 0g, Cholesterol: 0mg, Sodium: 150mg, Total Carbohydrates: 7g, Dietary Fiber: 2g, Sugars: 0g, Protein: 3g

Indulge in the goodness of this Butter Bean and Smoked Almond Dip, a wholesome and flavorful addition to your collection of healthy recipes.

69. Butter Bean and Cinnamon Hummus

Discover a delightful twist to traditional hummus with this Butter Bean and Cinnamon Hummus recipe. Butter beans, also known as Lima beans, add a creamy texture to the hummus, while a hint of cinnamon introduces a warm and aromatic flavor. Packed with protein and fiber, this unique hummus is a nutritious and delicious addition to your snack or appetizer repertoire. Embrace the goodness of butter beans in a new, flavorful way!

Serving: Makes approximately 2 cups of Butter Bean and Cinnamon Hummus.
Preparation Time: 15 minutes
Ready Time: 15 minutes

Ingredients:
- 1 can (15 ounces) butter beans, drained and rinsed
- 3 tablespoons tahini
- 2 tablespoons extra virgin olive oil
- 2 tablespoons fresh lemon juice
- 1 clove garlic, minced
- 1 teaspoon ground cinnamon
- 1/2 teaspoon cumin
- 1/2 teaspoon salt, or to taste
- 1/4 teaspoon black pepper
- 2-3 tablespoons water (adjust for desired consistency)
- Optional garnish: a drizzle of olive oil, a sprinkle of cinnamon, and a handful of chopped fresh parsley

Instructions:
1. In a food processor, combine the butter beans, tahini, olive oil, lemon juice, minced garlic, ground cinnamon, cumin, salt, and black pepper.
2. Blend the ingredients until smooth, scraping down the sides as needed to ensure even mixing.
3. While the processor is running, add water one tablespoon at a time until the hummus reaches your preferred consistency.
4. Taste the hummus and adjust the seasoning, adding more salt or lemon juice if needed.

5. Transfer the hummus to a serving bowl and drizzle with a bit of olive oil. Sprinkle with a touch of cinnamon and chopped fresh parsley for a finishing touch.

6. Serve the Butter Bean and Cinnamon Hummus with your favorite whole grain crackers, pita bread, or fresh vegetable sticks.

Nutrition Information:
Note: Nutrition values are approximate and may vary based on specific ingredients used.
- Serving Size: 2 tablespoons
- Calories: 60, Total Fat: 4g, Saturated Fat: 0.5g, Trans Fat: 0g, Cholesterol: 0mg, Sodium: 120mg, Total Carbohydrates: 5g, Dietary Fiber: 1g, Sugars: 0g, Protein: 2g

Enjoy this wholesome Butter Bean and Cinnamon Hummus as a nutritious snack or a crowd-pleasing appetizer at your next gathering!

70. Butter Bean and Pickled Jalapeño Dip

This zesty Butter Bean and Pickled Jalapeño Dip is a delightful twist on a classic bean dip, offering a flavorful and healthy option for your snacking needs. The creamy texture of butter beans combines with the bold kick of pickled jalapeños to create a satisfying dip that's perfect for parties or everyday enjoyment. Packed with protein and fiber, this dip not only tantalizes your taste buds but also provides a nutritious boost.

Serving: Makes approximately 2 cups of dip
Preparation Time: 15 minutes
Ready Time: 15 minutes

Ingredients:
- 1 can (15 ounces) butter beans, drained and rinsed
- 1/4 cup pickled jalapeños, chopped (adjust to taste)
- 2 cloves garlic, minced
- 2 tablespoons fresh lemon juice
- 2 tablespoons olive oil
- 1 teaspoon ground cumin
- Salt and pepper to taste
- 2 tablespoons fresh cilantro, chopped (for garnish)

Instructions:
1. In a food processor, combine the butter beans, pickled jalapeños, minced garlic, fresh lemon juice, olive oil, ground cumin, salt, and pepper.
2. Blend the ingredients until the mixture reaches a smooth and creamy consistency, scraping down the sides of the processor as needed.
3. Taste the dip and adjust the seasoning according to your preference, adding more salt, pepper, or jalapeños as desired.
4. Transfer the dip to a serving bowl and garnish with fresh chopped cilantro.
5. Serve the Butter Bean and Pickled Jalapeño Dip with an array of colorful vegetable sticks, whole-grain crackers, or pita bread for a healthy and satisfying snack.

Nutrition Information:
Note: Nutritional values are approximate and may vary based on specific ingredients and serving sizes.
- Serving Size: 2 tablespoons
- Calories: 60, Total Fat: 3g, Saturated Fat: 0.5g, Trans Fat: 0g, Cholesterol: 0mg, Sodium: 120mg, Total Carbohydrates: 7g, Dietary Fiber: 2g, Sugars: 0g, Protein: 2g

Enjoy this flavorful Butter Bean and Pickled Jalapeño Dip as a wholesome and delicious addition to your healthy snacking repertoire!

71. Butter Bean and Cashew Spread

Transform your ordinary butter beans into a delightful and nutritious spread with our Butter Bean and Cashew Spread recipe. Packed with protein, fiber, and healthy fats, this spread is not only delicious but also a versatile addition to your healthy eating repertoire. Whether you're looking for a savory dip for your veggies or a hearty sandwich spread, this recipe is sure to elevate your meals with a burst of flavor and wholesome goodness.

Serving: Makes approximately 1.5 cups of spread.
Preparation Time: 15 minutes
Ready Time: 20 minutes

Ingredients:
- 1 can (15 ounces) butter beans, drained and rinsed
- 1/2 cup raw cashews
- 2 cloves garlic, minced
- 3 tablespoons fresh lemon juice
- 2 tablespoons olive oil
- 1 tablespoon nutritional yeast
- 1 teaspoon ground cumin
- 1/2 teaspoon smoked paprika
- Salt and pepper to taste
- 2 tablespoons fresh parsley, chopped (for garnish)

Instructions:
1. In a food processor, combine the drained butter beans, raw cashews, minced garlic, fresh lemon juice, olive oil, nutritional yeast, ground cumin, smoked paprika, salt, and pepper.
2. Blend the ingredients until smooth and creamy, scraping down the sides of the food processor as needed to ensure everything is well combined.
3. Taste the spread and adjust the seasoning if necessary, adding more salt, pepper, or lemon juice according to your preference.
4. Once the spread reaches your desired consistency and flavor, transfer it to a serving bowl.
5. Garnish the Butter Bean and Cashew Spread with chopped fresh parsley for a burst of color and freshness.
6. Serve the spread with your favorite vegetable sticks, whole-grain crackers, or use it as a sandwich filling.

Nutrition Information:
Per serving (2 tablespoons):
- Calories: 80, Total Fat: 5g, Saturated Fat: 1g, Trans Fat: 0g, Cholesterol: 0mg, Sodium: 120mg, Total Carbohydrates: 7g, Dietary Fiber: 2g, Sugars: 1g, Protein: 3g

Note: Nutrition Information is approximate and may vary based on specific ingredients and serving sizes. Adjust quantities accordingly for your dietary preferences.

72. Butter Bean and Roasted Garlic Pesto

Elevate your culinary experience with this delightful and nutritious Butter Bean and Roasted Garlic Pesto. Butter beans, also known as Lima beans, take center stage in this recipe, offering a creamy texture and a wealth of health benefits. Paired with the rich flavors of roasted garlic and a vibrant pesto, this dish is a celebration of wholesome ingredients and bold taste. Perfect for those seeking a flavorful and healthy twist on traditional pesto, this recipe is a testament to the versatility of butter beans.

Serving: 4 servings
Preparation time: 15 minutes
Ready time: 45 minutes

Ingredients:
- 2 cups canned butter beans, drained and rinsed
- 1 head of garlic
- 1 cup fresh basil leaves, packed
- 1/2 cup grated Parmesan cheese
- 1/3 cup pine nuts, toasted
- 1/2 cup extra-virgin olive oil
- 1 tablespoon lemon juice
- Salt and pepper to taste
- Optional: red pepper flakes for a hint of heat

Instructions:
1. Roast the Garlic:
- Preheat the oven to 400°F (200°C).
- Cut the top off the head of garlic to expose the cloves.
- Drizzle with olive oil, wrap in aluminum foil, and roast for 30-40 minutes or until the garlic is soft and golden. Allow it to cool.
2. Prepare the Butter Beans:
- In a medium-sized pot, bring water to a boil.
- Add the butter beans and cook for 5-7 minutes or until tender.
- Drain and rinse the beans under cold water to stop the cooking process.
3. Make the Pesto:
- In a food processor, combine the roasted garlic cloves (squeeze them out of the skins), butter beans, basil, Parmesan cheese, pine nuts, and lemon juice.

- Pulse until the ingredients are finely chopped.
- With the food processor running, slowly pour in the olive oil until the pesto reaches a smooth consistency.
- Season with salt and pepper to taste. If you like a bit of heat, add red pepper flakes.

4. Serve:
- Toss the pesto with your favorite pasta or use it as a spread on whole-grain bread.
- Garnish with additional Parmesan cheese and a sprinkle of fresh basil.

5.

Nutrition Information:
- Per Serving:
- Calories: 320, Protein: 10g, Fat: 25g, Carbohydrates: 15g, Fiber: 5g

Note: Adjust the consistency of the pesto by adding more olive oil if desired. This Butter Bean and Roasted Garlic Pesto is a wholesome, protein-packed dish that's as delicious as it is nutritious. Enjoy the unique flavors and textures as you explore the healthy ways to incorporate butter beans into your culinary repertoire.

73. Butter Bean and Chili-Lime Salsa

This zesty Butter Bean and Chili-Lime Salsa dish is a vibrant, nutritious addition to any meal. Bursting with flavors of tangy lime, spicy chili, and creamy butter beans, it's a versatile salsa that can be used as a topping, dip, or side dish. Packed with protein, fiber, and essential nutrients, it's a delicious way to incorporate the goodness of butter beans into your diet.

Serving:
- Serves: 4-6

Preparation Time:
- Prep Time: 15 minutes

Ready Time:
- Ready In: 15 minutes

Ingredients:
- 2 cans (15 ounces each) butter beans, drained and rinsed
- 1 red bell pepper, diced
- 1 jalapeño pepper, finely chopped (seeds removed for milder taste)

- 1/4 cup red onion, finely chopped
- 2 cloves garlic, minced
- 1/4 cup fresh cilantro, chopped
- Zest and juice of 2 limes
- 2 tablespoons olive oil
- 1 teaspoon honey or agave syrup
- 1/2 teaspoon ground cumin
- Salt and pepper to taste
- Optional: Avocado slices for garnish

Instructions:
1. In a large mixing bowl, combine the drained and rinsed butter beans, diced red bell pepper, chopped jalapeño pepper, finely chopped red onion, minced garlic, and chopped cilantro.
2. In a separate small bowl, whisk together the lime zest, lime juice, olive oil, honey or agave syrup, ground cumin, salt, and pepper.
3. Pour the lime dressing over the butter bean mixture and gently toss until everything is evenly coated.
4. Taste and adjust seasoning, adding more salt, pepper, or lime juice if desired.
5. Allow the salsa to marinate for at least 10 minutes to let the flavors meld together.
6. Garnish with avocado slices if preferred before serving.

Nutrition Information
(per serving):
- Calories: Approximately 220 kcal, Protein: 9g, Carbohydrates: 31g, Fat: 7g, Fiber: 9g, Sodium: 410mg
- Potassium: 660mg

Note: Nutritional values are approximate and may vary based on specific ingredients used.

Enjoy this Butter Bean and Chili-Lime Salsa as a topping for tacos, a side dish with grilled chicken or fish, or simply as a refreshing dip with your favorite tortilla chips. It's a delightful and healthy way to savor the goodness of butter beans in a flavorful ensemble.

74. Butter Bean and Paprika Dip

This delectable Butter Bean and Paprika Dip is a delightful addition to any table, offering a burst of flavors and a creamy texture that perfectly complements various dishes. Packed with the wholesome goodness of butter beans and the smoky richness of paprika, this dip is a nutritious and flavorful option for snack time or as an appetizer for gatherings.

Serving: Serves 6-8 people as a dip or spread.
Preparation time: 10 minutes
Ready time: 15 minutes

Ingredients:
- 2 cans (15 ounces each) butter beans, drained and rinsed
- 3 cloves garlic, minced
- 2 tablespoons olive oil
- 1 tablespoon lemon juice
- 1 teaspoon smoked paprika
- ½ teaspoon ground cumin
- Salt and black pepper to taste
- 2 tablespoons chopped fresh parsley (optional, for garnish)

Instructions:
1. Prepare the butter beans by draining and rinsing them thoroughly under cold water. Drain well.
2. In a food processor, combine the butter beans, minced garlic, olive oil, lemon juice, smoked paprika, ground cumin, salt, and black pepper.
3. Blend the ingredients until smooth and creamy, scraping down the sides of the processor as needed to ensure everything is well combined. If the dip seems too thick, you can add a splash of water or more olive oil for desired consistency.
4. Taste the dip and adjust seasonings according to your preference by adding more salt, pepper, or lemon juice if needed.
5. Once the dip reaches the desired consistency and taste, transfer it to a serving bowl. If desired, garnish with chopped fresh parsley for a pop of color and added freshness.
6. Serve the Butter Bean and Paprika Dip with a variety of accompaniments such as fresh vegetables, pita bread, whole-grain crackers, or as a spread on sandwiches.

Nutrition Information
(per serving - estimated):
- Calories: 120, Total Fat: 5g, Saturated Fat: 0.7g, Cholesterol: 0mg, Sodium: 190mg, Total Carbohydrates: 15g, Dietary Fiber: 4g, Sugars: 0.5g, Protein: 5g

Note: Nutritional values are approximate and may vary based on specific ingredients used and serving sizes.

Enjoy this flavorful and nutritious Butter Bean and Paprika Dip as a wholesome addition to your meals or as a standalone snack!

75. Butter Bean and Mango Chutney

Welcome to the world of nutritious and versatile butter beans! This recipe combines the wholesome goodness of butter beans with the vibrant flavors of mango chutney. The sweet and tangy notes of mango perfectly complement the creamy texture of butter beans, creating a dish that's both delicious and packed with essential nutrients.

Serving: 4 servings
Preparation time: 10 minutes
Ready time: 20 minutes

Ingredients:
- 2 cans (15 ounces each) butter beans, drained and rinsed
- 1 ripe mango, peeled and diced
- 1 small red onion, finely chopped
- 2 cloves garlic, minced
- 1 tablespoon fresh ginger, grated
- 1 tablespoon olive oil
- 2 tablespoons apple cider vinegar
- 2 tablespoons honey or maple syrup
- 1 teaspoon ground cumin
- 1/2 teaspoon ground turmeric
- Salt and pepper to taste
- Fresh cilantro for garnish (optional)

Instructions:
1. Prepare the Mango Chutney:

- In a saucepan, heat olive oil over medium heat. Add chopped onions and cook until they turn translucent, about 3-4 minutes.
- Stir in minced garlic and grated ginger, and cook for an additional 1-2 minutes until fragrant.
- Add diced mango, apple cider vinegar, honey or maple syrup, ground cumin, ground turmeric, salt, and pepper. Stir well to combine.
- Allow the mixture to simmer gently for 8-10 minutes, stirring occasionally, until the mango softens and the flavors meld together. Remove from heat and set aside.

2. Prepare the Butter Beans:
- In a separate pan, add the drained and rinsed butter beans.
- Warm the beans over medium heat for 3-4 minutes, stirring occasionally.

3. Combine and Serve:
- Once the beans are warm, pour the prepared mango chutney over the butter beans in the pan.
- Gently stir to coat the beans with the chutney mixture.
- Allow it to simmer together for an additional 2-3 minutes to let the flavors infuse.
- Taste and adjust seasoning if needed.
- Garnish with fresh cilantro, if desired, before serving.

Nutrition Information: (per serving)
- Calories: 240 kcal, Total Fat: 4g, Saturated Fat: 0.5g, Cholesterol: 0mg, Sodium: 410mg
- Total Carbohydrate: 44g, Dietary Fiber: 10g, Sugars: 15g, Protein: 10g

Enjoy this delightful Butter Bean and Mango Chutney dish as a flavorful side or a main course, and relish the nutritious blend of butter beans and tangy mango goodness!

76. Butter Bean and Roasted Bell Pepper Hummus

Transforming the traditional hummus recipe, this Butter Bean and Roasted Bell Pepper Hummus is a delightful twist that champions the goodness of butter beans. It's a fusion of flavors, blending the creaminess of butter beans with the smoky sweetness of roasted bell peppers. This nutritious dip is not only delicious but also a versatile addition to any meal or snack.

Serving: 8 servings
Preparation time: 15 minutes
Ready time: 25 minutes

Ingredients:
- 1 can (15 ounces) butter beans, drained and rinsed
- 2 roasted red bell peppers, peeled and seeded
- 3 tablespoons tahini
- 2 cloves garlic, minced
- 3 tablespoons fresh lemon juice
- 2 tablespoons olive oil
- 1 teaspoon ground cumin
- Salt and pepper to taste
- Optional: Chopped fresh parsley or paprika for garnish
- Whole grain pita bread or vegetable sticks for serving

Instructions:
1. Preheat the oven to 400°F (200°C). Place the whole red bell peppers on a baking sheet and roast in the oven for 20-25 minutes until the skin is charred and blistered. Remove from the oven and place the peppers in a bowl, covering it with plastic wrap. Let them cool for 10 minutes, then peel off the skin, remove the seeds, and chop the flesh roughly.
2. In a food processor, combine the butter beans, roasted bell peppers, tahini, minced garlic, lemon juice, olive oil, cumin, salt, and pepper.
3. Blend the mixture until smooth and creamy. If the hummus is too thick, add a tablespoon of water or extra olive oil to reach your desired consistency. Taste and adjust seasonings if needed.
4. Transfer the hummus to a serving bowl. Drizzle with a little extra olive oil and garnish with chopped parsley or a sprinkle of paprika for an extra pop of color and flavor.
5. Serve the Butter Bean and Roasted Bell Pepper Hummus with whole grain pita bread wedges or fresh vegetable sticks for a healthy and delicious snack or appetizer.

Nutrition Information
(per serving, approximately 2 tablespoons):
- Calories: 90, Total Fat: 6g, Saturated Fat: 1g, Sodium: 110mg, Total Carbohydrates: 7g, Dietary Fiber: 2g, Sugars: 1g, Protein: 3g
Note: Nutrition Information may vary based on specific ingredients used and serving sizes.

77. Butter Bean and Black Bean Salsa

This zesty Butter Bean and Black Bean Salsa is a vibrant addition to any table, offering a burst of flavors and a healthy punch. Packed with protein, fiber, and essential nutrients from butter beans and black beans, this salsa is as nutritious as it is delicious. Perfect as a side dish, a topping for tacos, or a dip with crunchy tortilla chips, it's a versatile recipe that celebrates the goodness of butter beans in a delightful way.

Serving: Makes about 4 cups of salsa
Preparation time: 15 minutes
Ready time: 15 minutes

Ingredients:
- 1 can (15 oz) butter beans, drained and rinsed
- 1 can (15 oz) black beans, drained and rinsed
- 1 red bell pepper, diced
- 1 green bell pepper, diced
- 1 small red onion, finely chopped
- 1 jalapeño pepper, seeded and minced (optional for heat)
- 1/4 cup fresh cilantro, chopped
- 2 tablespoons olive oil
- Juice of 2 limes
- Salt and pepper to taste
- 1 teaspoon ground cumin
- Tortilla chips for serving (optional)

Instructions:
1. In a large mixing bowl, combine the drained and rinsed butter beans and black beans.
2. Add the diced red and green bell peppers, finely chopped red onion, minced jalapeño (if using), and chopped cilantro to the bowl.
3. In a separate small bowl, whisk together the olive oil, lime juice, salt, pepper, and ground cumin to create the dressing.
4. Pour the dressing over the bean mixture and gently toss until well combined.
5. Taste and adjust seasoning if needed. For enhanced flavors, allow the salsa to marinate in the refrigerator for at least 15 minutes before serving.

6. Serve chilled as a salsa with tortilla chips or as a topping for tacos, grilled meats, or salads.

Nutrition Information: (per 1/2 cup serving)
- Calories: 120, Total Fat: 4g, Saturated Fat: 0.5g, Trans Fat: 0g, Cholesterol: 0mg, Sodium: 180mg, Total Carbohydrates: 17g, Dietary Fiber: 5g, Sugars: 1g, Protein: 6g
- Vitamin D: 0%
- Calcium: 4%
- Iron: 10%
- Potassium: 6%

This Butter Bean and Black Bean Salsa is not only a flavorful dish but also a nutritional powerhouse, providing a boost of energy and essential nutrients in every serving. Enjoy its freshness and versatility in various meal settings!

78. Butter Bean and Ginger Dip

Elevate your snacking experience with this delightful Butter Bean and Ginger Dip. Packed with protein and fiber, butter beans serve as the star ingredient in this healthy and flavorful dip. The addition of fresh ginger adds a zesty kick, making it a perfect companion for your favorite veggies or whole-grain crackers. Whip up this easy-to-make dip for a nutritious and satisfying treat.

Serving: Makes approximately 2 cups of dip.
Preparation Time: 15 minutes
Ready Time: 15 minutes

Ingredients:
- 1 can (15 ounces) butter beans, drained and rinsed
- 2 tablespoons tahini
- 2 tablespoons olive oil
- 1 tablespoon fresh lemon juice
- 1 teaspoon grated fresh ginger
- 2 cloves garlic, minced
- 1/2 teaspoon ground cumin
- Salt and pepper to taste

- 2 tablespoons chopped fresh parsley (for garnish)

Instructions:
1. In a food processor, combine the butter beans, tahini, olive oil, lemon juice, grated ginger, minced garlic, cumin, salt, and pepper.
2. Blend the ingredients until smooth and creamy, scraping down the sides of the processor as needed.
3. Taste and adjust the seasoning as desired, adding more salt, pepper, or lemon juice.
4. Transfer the dip to a serving bowl and garnish with chopped fresh parsley.
5. Serve with an assortment of fresh vegetables, such as carrot sticks, cucumber slices, and bell pepper strips, or whole-grain crackers.

Nutrition Information:
(Per 2-tablespoon serving)
- Calories: 70, Protein: 2g, Fat: 5g, Carbohydrates: 5g, Fiber: 2g, Sugars: 0g, Sodium: 90mg

Indulge in this Butter Bean and Ginger Dip guilt-free, knowing that you're treating your taste buds to a healthy and wholesome snack.

79. Butter Bean and Roasted Butternut Squash Hummus

Elevate your snacking experience with this nutritious and delicious Butter Bean and Roasted Butternut Squash Hummus. Packed with the wholesome goodness of butter beans and the earthy sweetness of roasted butternut squash, this hummus is a delightful twist on the classic recipe. Not only does it offer a creamy and satisfying texture, but it also adds a burst of color and flavor to your table. Enjoy guilt-free indulgence with this protein-rich and fiber-packed dip that's perfect for spreading on whole-grain crackers or dipping your favorite veggies.

Serving: Makes approximately 2 cups of hummus.
Preparation Time: 15 minutes
Ready Time: 45 minutes (including roasting time for butternut squash)

Ingredients:

- 1 can (15 oz) butter beans, drained and rinsed
- 1 cup roasted butternut squash, peeled and diced
- 2 cloves garlic, minced
- 3 tablespoons tahini
- 2 tablespoons extra virgin olive oil
- Juice of 1 lemon
- 1 teaspoon ground cumin
- 1/2 teaspoon smoked paprika
- Salt and pepper to taste
- Water (as needed for desired consistency)

Instructions:
1. Preheat the oven to 400°F (200°C).
2. Peel and dice the butternut squash, removing seeds.
3. Place the diced butternut squash on a baking sheet, drizzle with olive oil, and sprinkle with salt and pepper. Roast in the preheated oven for 30-35 minutes or until tender and lightly browned. Allow it to cool.
4. In a food processor, combine the butter beans, roasted butternut squash, minced garlic, tahini, olive oil, lemon juice, ground cumin, smoked paprika, salt, and pepper.
5. Process the mixture until smooth, adding water as needed to achieve your desired consistency.
6. Taste and adjust seasoning if necessary.
7. Transfer the hummus to a serving bowl and drizzle with a bit of olive oil.
8. Serve with whole-grain crackers, pita bread, or fresh vegetable sticks.

Nutrition Information:
(Per 2-tablespoon serving)
- Calories: 50, Total Fat: 3g, Saturated Fat: 0.4g, Cholesterol: 0mg, Sodium: 80mg, Total Carbohydrates: 5g, Dietary Fiber: 1.5g, Sugars: 0.5g, Protein: 2g

Enjoy this Butter Bean and Roasted Butternut Squash Hummus as a wholesome snack or a flavorful addition to your meals, providing a healthy dose of nutrients and a burst of deliciousness.

80. Butter Bean and Saffron Aioli

Elevate your culinary experience with this delightful recipe that combines the wholesome goodness of butter beans with the aromatic allure of saffron-infused aioli. Butter Bean and Saffron Aioli is a harmonious marriage of textures and flavors, creating a dish that not only tantalizes the taste buds but also offers a healthy twist to your dining table. Packed with protein and fiber, this recipe showcases the versatility of butter beans in a dish that is as visually stunning as it is delicious.

Serving: 4 servings
Preparation time: 15 minutes
Ready time: 30 minutes

Ingredients:
- 2 cups cooked butter beans (canned or soaked and boiled)
- 1/4 teaspoon saffron threads
- 2 tablespoons hot water
- 1 cup mayonnaise (preferably low-fat)
- 2 cloves garlic, minced
- 1 tablespoon lemon juice
- Salt and pepper to taste
- 2 tablespoons fresh parsley, chopped (for garnish)

Instructions:
1. Prepare the Saffron Aioli:
- In a small bowl, steep saffron threads in hot water. Allow it to sit for 5-10 minutes until the water turns a rich golden hue.
- In a separate mixing bowl, combine mayonnaise, minced garlic, lemon juice, and the saffron-infused water. Whisk until well blended.
- Season with salt and pepper to taste. Set aside.

2. Cook Butter Beans:
- If using canned butter beans, drain and rinse them thoroughly. If using dried beans, ensure they are soaked and boiled until tender.
- Allow the butter beans to cool to room temperature.

3. Combine Butter Beans and Saffron Aioli:
- Gently fold the cooked butter beans into the saffron aioli, ensuring each bean is coated with the flavorful sauce.

4. Chill and Serve:
- Refrigerate the Butter Bean and Saffron Aioli for at least 15 minutes to allow the flavors to meld.
- Serve chilled, garnished with fresh chopped parsley for a burst of color and added freshness.

Nutrition Information
(per serving):
- Calories: 220 kcal, Protein: 8g, Fat: 15g, Carbohydrates: 18g, Fiber: 6g, Sugars: 2g, Sodium: 280mg
Note: Adjustments to serving sizes and nutritional information may vary based on specific brands and quantities of ingredients used.

81. Butter Bean and Black Olive Hummus

Elevate your snacking experience with this wholesome Butter Bean and Black Olive Hummus, a delightful twist on the classic chickpea-based dip. Butter beans, known for their creamy texture and rich flavor, blend harmoniously with the briny essence of black olives, creating a dip that's not only delicious but also packed with nutrition. Perfect for dipping veggies, spreading on whole-grain crackers, or as a flavorful addition to wraps, this hummus is a versatile and healthy option for any occasion.

Serving: Makes approximately 2 cups of hummus.
Preparation Time: 15 minutes
Ready Time: 15 minutes

Ingredients:
- 1 can (15 ounces) butter beans, drained and rinsed
- 1/2 cup black olives, pitted and sliced
- 1/4 cup tahini
- 2 cloves garlic, minced
- 2 tablespoons extra-virgin olive oil
- 2 tablespoons fresh lemon juice
- 1 teaspoon ground cumin
- 1/2 teaspoon paprika
- Salt and pepper to taste
- Water (as needed for desired consistency)
- Optional garnish: chopped fresh parsley, extra olive oil, and a sprinkle of paprika

Instructions:

1. In a food processor, combine the butter beans, black olives, tahini, minced garlic, olive oil, lemon juice, ground cumin, paprika, salt, and pepper.
2. Blend the ingredients until smooth, scraping down the sides of the processor as needed.
3. If the hummus is too thick, add water, one tablespoon at a time, until you reach your desired consistency.
4. Taste and adjust the seasonings as needed, adding more salt, pepper, or lemon juice to suit your preference.
5. Once the hummus is smooth and well-balanced, transfer it to a serving bowl.
6. Optionally, garnish with chopped fresh parsley, a drizzle of extra olive oil, and a sprinkle of paprika.
7. Serve the Butter Bean and Black Olive Hummus with an array of fresh vegetables, whole-grain crackers, or use it as a spread in wraps.

Nutrition Information:
(Per 2-tablespoon serving)
- Calories: 60, Total Fat: 4g, Saturated Fat: 0.5g, Cholesterol: 0mg, Sodium: 120mg, Total Carbohydrates: 5g, Dietary Fiber: 1g, Sugars: 0g, Protein: 2g

This Butter Bean and Black Olive Hummus is not only a flavorful addition to your snacking repertoire but also a nutritious choice that aligns with a healthy lifestyle. Enjoy the rich, creamy goodness guilt-free!

82. Butter Bean and Cranberry Salsa

Indulge in the wholesome goodness of our Butter Bean and Cranberry Salsa—a delightful twist on traditional salsa recipes that packs a punch of flavor and nutrition. Butter beans, also known as lima beans, are the star of this dish, bringing a creamy texture and a boost of protein to the table. Paired with the tartness of cranberries and a medley of vibrant vegetables, this salsa is a celebration of health and taste. Perfect as a side dish, topping, or even a standalone snack, it's a versatile addition to your repertoire of healthy recipes.

Serving: This recipe serves 4.
Preparation Time: 15 minutes

Ready Time: 15 minutes

Ingredients:
- 2 cups cooked butter beans (canned or cooked from dry)
- 1 cup fresh cranberries, chopped
- 1/2 cup red onion, finely diced
- 1/2 cup red bell pepper, diced
- 1/4 cup fresh cilantro, chopped
- 1 jalapeño, seeds removed and finely chopped
- 1 clove garlic, minced
- Juice of 2 limes
- 2 tablespoons olive oil
- Salt and pepper to taste

Instructions:
1. In a large mixing bowl, combine the cooked butter beans, chopped cranberries, diced red onion, red bell pepper, cilantro, jalapeño, and minced garlic.
2. In a small bowl, whisk together the lime juice and olive oil. Pour the dressing over the bean mixture.
3. Gently toss all the ingredients together until well combined. Season with salt and pepper to taste.
4. Allow the salsa to marinate for at least 10 minutes to let the flavors meld.
5. Serve chilled as a side dish, topping for grilled meats or fish, or as a healthy dip with whole-grain tortilla chips.

Nutrition Information:
Note: Nutrition Information is per serving.
- Calories: 220, Protein: 9g, Carbohydrates: 30g, Fiber: 8g, Sugars: 5g, Fat: 8g, Saturated Fat: 1g, Cholesterol: 0mg, Sodium: 180mg
Enjoy the vibrant, nutritious goodness of Butter Bean and Cranberry Salsa as a delicious and guilt-free addition to your healthy eating journey!

83. Butter Bean and Walnut Pesto

Explore the versatility of butter beans with this delightful and nutritious Butter Bean and Walnut Pesto recipe. Butter beans, also known as lima beans, add a creamy texture to this pesto, while the richness of walnuts enhances both the flavor and nutritional profile. This healthy twist on traditional pesto offers a protein-packed, fiber-rich alternative that's as delicious as it is wholesome. Enjoy it as a spread, pasta sauce, or a vibrant dip—the possibilities are endless!

Serving: Makes approximately 1 cup of pesto.
Preparation Time: 15 minutes
Ready Time: 15 minutes

Ingredients:
- 1 can (15 oz) butter beans, drained and rinsed
- 1 cup fresh basil leaves, packed
- 1/2 cup walnuts, toasted
- 1/2 cup grated Parmesan cheese
- 2 cloves garlic, minced
- 1/2 cup extra-virgin olive oil
- Juice of 1 lemon
- Salt and pepper to taste

Instructions:
1. Prepare Ingredients: Drain and rinse the butter beans. Toast the walnuts in a dry pan over medium heat until fragrant, about 3-5 minutes. Allow them to cool.
2. Blend Ingredients: In a food processor, combine the butter beans, basil, toasted walnuts, Parmesan cheese, and minced garlic. Pulse until the mixture is coarsely chopped.
3. Add Olive Oil and Lemon Juice: With the food processor running, slowly stream in the olive oil and lemon juice until the pesto reaches your desired consistency. Stop and scrape down the sides as needed.
4. Season: Add salt and pepper to taste. Blend again until well combined.
5. Adjust Consistency: If the pesto is too thick, you can add more olive oil to achieve the desired texture.
6. Serve: Use the Butter Bean and Walnut Pesto as a spread on whole grain bread, toss it with cooked pasta, or serve as a dip with fresh vegetables.

Nutrition Information:
(Per 2 tablespoons)

- Calories: 120, Total Fat: 10g, Saturated Fat: 2g, Trans Fat: 0g, Cholesterol: 5mg, Sodium: 90mg, Total Carbohydrates: 5g, Dietary Fiber: 2g, Sugars: 0g, Protein: 4g

Enjoy this Butter Bean and Walnut Pesto guilt-free, knowing that every bite is packed with flavor and nutritional goodness.

84. Butter Bean and Pomegranate Salsa

Indulge in a burst of flavors and nourishment with this vibrant Butter Bean and Pomegranate Salsa. This recipe not only celebrates the wholesome goodness of butter beans but also combines them with the refreshing sweetness of pomegranate seeds, creating a salsa that's as delightful as it is nutritious. Bursting with antioxidants, fiber, and protein, this dish exemplifies the epitome of healthy eating without compromising on taste. Perfect as a side dish, topping, or even a standalone snack, this salsa is a testament to the endless possibilities of incorporating butter beans into your culinary repertoire.

Serving: 4 servings
Preparation Time: 15 minutes
Ready Time: 15 minutes

Ingredients:
- 2 cups cooked butter beans, drained and rinsed
- 1 cup pomegranate seeds
- 1/2 red onion, finely diced
- 1 cucumber, diced
- 1/4 cup fresh cilantro, chopped
- 1 jalapeño, finely chopped (seeds removed for milder salsa)
- 2 tablespoons extra-virgin olive oil
- 1 tablespoon lime juice
- Salt and pepper to taste

Instructions:
1. In a large bowl, combine the butter beans, pomegranate seeds, red onion, cucumber, cilantro, and jalapeño.
2. In a small bowl, whisk together the olive oil and lime juice to create the dressing.

3. Pour the dressing over the bean mixture and gently toss until well combined.
4. Season with salt and pepper to taste.
5. Allow the salsa to marinate for at least 15 minutes to let the flavors meld.
6. Serve chilled as a side dish, topping for grilled proteins, or with whole-grain chips for a healthy snack.

Nutrition Information
(per serving):
- Calories: 210, Protein: 8g, Carbohydrates: 30g, Fiber: 8g, Sugars: 8g, Fat: 8g, Saturated Fat: 1g, Cholesterol: 0mg, Sodium: 15mg
Note: Nutrition Information is approximate and may vary based on specific ingredients used.

85. Butter Bean and Roasted Jalapeño Hummus

Indulge in a wholesome and flavorful journey with our Butter Bean and Roasted Jalapeño Hummus. This innovative take on traditional hummus introduces butter beans, packing a protein punch while maintaining a velvety texture. The addition of roasted jalapeños adds a smoky kick, elevating this dip to a whole new level. Perfect for those seeking healthy and delicious alternatives, this recipe embodies the essence of our cookbook, "Healthy The Ways to Use Butter Beans Recipes."

Serving: Makes approximately 2 cups of hummus.
Preparation Time: 15 minutes
Ready Time: 45 minutes (including roasting time for jalapeños)

Ingredients:
- 2 cups cooked butter beans (canned or cooked from dried)
- 2-3 jalapeños, roasted
- 3 tablespoons tahini
- 2 cloves garlic, minced
- 1/4 cup extra-virgin olive oil
- Juice of 1 lemon
- 1 teaspoon ground cumin
- Salt and pepper to taste

- 2 tablespoons water (adjust for desired consistency)
- Optional toppings: drizzle of olive oil, paprika, chopped fresh cilantro

Instructions:
1. Roast Jalapeños:
- Preheat the oven to 400°F (200°C).
- Place whole jalapeños on a baking sheet and roast for 20-25 minutes, turning occasionally until the skin is charred.
- Remove from the oven, place in a bowl, and cover with plastic wrap to let them steam. Once cooled, peel, deseed, and chop.
2. Prepare Butter Beans:
- If using canned butter beans, drain and rinse them. If using dried beans, cook them according to package instructions until soft.
3. Blend

Ingredients:
- In a food processor, combine the butter beans, roasted jalapeños, tahini, minced garlic, olive oil, lemon juice, cumin, salt, and pepper.
- Blend until smooth, adding water gradually to achieve your preferred consistency.
4. Adjust Seasoning:
- Taste the hummus and adjust seasoning if needed. Add more salt, pepper, or lemon juice according to your preference.
5. Serve:
- Transfer the hummus to a serving bowl. Drizzle with olive oil, sprinkle with paprika, and garnish with chopped cilantro if desired.
6.

Nutrition Information:
- (Per 2 tablespoons)
- Calories: 80, Protein: 3g, Fat: 6g, Carbohydrates: 5g, Fiber: 2g, Sugar: 0g, Sodium: 80mg
Note: Nutrition Information is approximate and may vary based on specific ingredients and serving sizes.

Indulge guilt-free in this Butter Bean and Roasted Jalapeño Hummus, a versatile delight perfect for dipping, spreading, or even as a flavorful topping. Healthy and delicious, it's a testament to the diverse ways butter beans can be enjoyed.

86. Butter Bean and Curry Dip

This Butter Bean and Curry Dip recipe is a delightful addition to your repertoire of healthy and versatile butter bean dishes. Blending the creamy texture of butter beans with aromatic curry spices creates a flavorful dip perfect for snacking or as a side for your favorite meals. Packed with nutrients and protein, it's a delicious way to incorporate more legumes into your diet.

Serving:
Serves: 6-8
Preparation Time:
Prep: 10 minutes
Ready Time:
Ready in: 15 minutes

Ingredients:
- 2 cans (15 oz each) butter beans, drained and rinsed
- 2 tablespoons olive oil
- 2 cloves garlic, minced
- 1 teaspoon curry powder
- 1/2 teaspoon ground cumin
- 1/2 teaspoon ground coriander
- 1/4 teaspoon turmeric
- Juice of 1 lemon
- Salt and pepper to taste
- Chopped fresh cilantro for garnish (optional)

Instructions:
1. Prepare Beans: Rinse and drain the butter beans thoroughly.
2. Sauté Aromatics: In a skillet over medium heat, add olive oil. Sauté minced garlic until fragrant, about 1-2 minutes.
3. Add Spices: Stir in curry powder, ground cumin, ground coriander, and turmeric. Cook for an additional minute, allowing the spices to bloom.
4. Blend Ingredients: In a food processor or blender, combine the sautéed spices, garlic, butter beans, lemon juice, salt, and pepper.
5. Blend to Smooth Consistency: Blend until smooth and creamy, scraping down the sides as needed. Adjust seasoning according to taste preferences.

6. Serve: Transfer the dip to a serving bowl. Garnish with chopped fresh cilantro if desired.

Nutrition Information:
Note: Nutritional values are approximate and may vary depending on specific ingredients used.
- Serving Size: 1/4 cup
- Calories: 120, Total Fat: 5g, Saturated Fat: 1g, Trans Fat: 0g, Cholesterol: 0mg, Sodium: 200mg, Total Carbohydrates: 15g, Dietary Fiber: 4g, Sugars: 1g, Protein: 5g

Enjoy this nutritious Butter Bean and Curry Dip with your favorite vegetables, pita chips, or as a spread in sandwiches. It's a versatile and healthy addition to any meal or snack time!

87. Butter Bean and Salsa Verde

Butter beans, with their creamy texture and versatility, are a delight in this vibrant Butter Bean and Salsa Verde recipe. Infused with the zesty flavors of salsa verde, this dish elevates the humble butter bean to a vibrant, nutritious delight. Perfect for those seeking healthy and flavorful meals, this recipe offers a burst of freshness in every bite.

Serving:
Serves: 4-6
Preparation time:
Prep: 15 minutes
Ready time:
Ready in: 25 minutes

Ingredients:
- 2 cans (15 ounces each) butter beans, drained and rinsed
- 1 cup fresh cilantro, finely chopped
- 1/2 cup fresh parsley, finely chopped
- 2 cloves garlic, minced
- 2 tablespoons capers, drained
- 1/4 cup extra-virgin olive oil
- 2 tablespoons fresh lemon juice
- 1 teaspoon lemon zest

- Salt and pepper to taste

Instructions:
1. Prepare the Salsa Verde:
- In a food processor, combine the cilantro, parsley, garlic, capers, olive oil, lemon juice, and lemon zest. Pulse until the mixture forms a coarse paste. Season with salt and pepper to taste. Set aside.
2. Cook the Butter Beans:
- In a saucepan, bring water to a boil. Add the drained and rinsed butter beans and cook for 3-4 minutes until they're heated through. Drain and transfer to a serving bowl.
3. Combine Beans and Salsa Verde:
- Pour the prepared salsa verde over the warm butter beans. Gently toss until the beans are evenly coated with the flavorful salsa verde mixture.
4. Serve:
- Serve the Butter Bean and Salsa Verde dish warm or at room temperature. Garnish with extra chopped cilantro or a drizzle of olive oil if desired.

Nutrition Information:
- Serving Size: 1/4 of recipe
- Calories: Approximately 250, Total Fat: 12g, Saturated Fat: 2g, Cholesterol: 0mg, Sodium: 400mg, Total Carbohydrates: 29g, Dietary Fiber: 9g, Sugars: 1g, Protein: 9g

Note: Nutrition Information is approximate and may vary based on specific ingredients used.

This Butter Bean and Salsa Verde recipe is a delightful addition to any table, providing a healthy and flavorful option for those seeking nutritious meal ideas. Enjoy the vibrant fusion of butter beans and zesty salsa verde for a satisfying and wholesome dish.

88. Butter Bean and Pineapple Salsa

This Butter Bean and Pineapple Salsa is a delightful fusion of flavors and textures that brings a burst of freshness to any meal. Butter beans, known for their creamy texture, combine beautifully with the sweetness of pineapple and the zing of fresh herbs. Enjoy this versatile salsa as a topping, a side, or a standalone snack—it's a nutritious and vibrant addition to your table.

Serving:
Serves: 4-6
Preparation time:
Prep: 15 minutes
Ready time:
Ready in: 15 minutes

Ingredients:
- 1 can (15 oz) butter beans, rinsed and drained
- 1 cup fresh pineapple, diced
- 1/2 red onion, finely chopped
- 1 red bell pepper, diced
- 1 jalapeño, seeded and finely chopped (optional for heat)
- 1/4 cup fresh cilantro, chopped
- Juice of 1 lime
- 2 tablespoons olive oil
- Salt and pepper to taste

Instructions:
1. In a mixing bowl, combine the rinsed and drained butter beans, diced pineapple, chopped red onion, diced red bell pepper, and jalapeño (if using).
2. Add the freshly chopped cilantro to the bowl.
For a milder salsa, soak the chopped onions in cold water for 10 minutes before adding them to the mix.
3. Drizzle the lime juice and olive oil over the mixture.
4. Gently toss the ingredients together until well combined.
5. Season with salt and pepper to taste.
6. Allow the flavors to meld by refrigerating the salsa for at least 15 minutes before serving.

Nutrition Information:
Per serving (assuming 4 servings)
- Calories: 180, Total Fat: 7g, Saturated Fat: 1g, Cholesterol: 0mg, Sodium: 280mg
- Total Carbohydrate: 25g, Dietary Fiber: 6g, Sugars: 7g, Protein: 6g

This vibrant salsa offers a burst of nutrients with its combination of protein-packed butter beans, vitamin-rich pineapple, and antioxidant-filled bell peppers. Enjoy it as a topping for grilled chicken or fish, as a dip for crunchy veggies, or simply on its own for a healthy, flavorful snack!

89. Butter Bean and Hazelnut Pesto

Explore the delightful world of healthy eating with this Butter Bean and Hazelnut Pesto recipe. Butter beans, with their creamy texture and nutty flavor, take center stage in this nutritious and delicious pesto. Combined with the rich, earthy notes of hazelnuts, this recipe is a delightful twist on traditional pesto, offering a satisfying and wholesome alternative. Perfect for those seeking both flavor and nourishment, this dish is a testament to the versatility of butter beans in creating vibrant, health-conscious meals.

Serving: 4 servings
Preparation Time: 15 minutes
Ready Time: 20 minutes

Ingredients:
- 1 can (15 ounces) butter beans, drained and rinsed
- 1/2 cup hazelnuts, toasted
- 2 cups fresh basil leaves, packed
- 3 cloves garlic, minced
- 1/2 cup grated Parmesan cheese
- 1/2 cup extra-virgin olive oil
- Salt and pepper to taste
- Juice of 1 lemon

Instructions:
1. Toast Hazelnuts: Preheat the oven to 350°F (175°C). Spread the hazelnuts on a baking sheet and toast them in the oven for about 8-10 minutes or until fragrant. Remove and let them cool.
2. Prepare Pesto Base: In a food processor, combine the butter beans, toasted hazelnuts, basil leaves, minced garlic, and Parmesan cheese.
3. Blend: Pulse the ingredients while gradually adding the olive oil until the mixture reaches a smooth and creamy consistency. If needed, scrape

down the sides of the processor with a spatula to ensure all ingredients are well incorporated.
4. Season: Add salt and pepper to taste. Squeeze in the juice of one lemon to brighten up the flavors, and blend again until everything is well combined.
5. Adjust Consistency: If the pesto is too thick, you can add more olive oil in small increments until you achieve your desired consistency.
6. Serve: Spoon the Butter Bean and Hazelnut Pesto over cooked pasta, grilled vegetables, or as a spread on whole-grain toast. Garnish with additional Parmesan cheese and a sprinkle of chopped hazelnuts if desired.

Nutrition Information
(per serving):
- Calories: 350, Protein: 10g, Fat: 30g, Carbohydrates: 12g, Fiber: 4g, Sugar: 1g, Sodium: 200mg

Indulge in this nutritious and flavorful Butter Bean and Hazelnut Pesto, celebrating the goodness of butter beans in a way that's both satisfying and health-conscious.

90. Butter Bean and Mango Salsa Verde

In this vibrant recipe, the buttery richness of beans meets the tangy sweetness of mango in a refreshing salsa verde. This dish celebrates the versatility of butter beans, offering a delightful twist that combines their creamy texture with the freshness of a homemade salsa.

Serving: 4 servings
Preparation time: 15 minutes
Ready time: 20 minutes

Ingredients:
- 2 cups cooked butter beans (canned or soaked and boiled)
- 1 ripe mango, diced
- 1/2 red onion, finely chopped
- 1 jalapeño pepper, seeded and minced
- 1/4 cup fresh cilantro, chopped
- 2 tablespoons fresh lime juice
- 2 tablespoons olive oil

- Salt and pepper to taste

Instructions:
1. Prepare the Beans: If using canned beans, drain and rinse them thoroughly. If using dried beans, soak them overnight, then boil until tender. Set aside to cool.
2. Prepare the Salsa Verde: In a mixing bowl, combine the diced mango, chopped red onion, minced jalapeño pepper, and chopped cilantro.
3. Mix In the Beans: Gently fold in the cooked butter beans with the salsa verde mixture.
4. Add Dressing: Drizzle the lime juice and olive oil over the salsa and beans. Toss gently to coat everything evenly.
5. Season to Taste: Season with salt and pepper according to your taste preferences.
6. Chill and Serve: For optimal flavor, refrigerate the butter bean and mango salsa verde for about 10-15 minutes before serving. This allows the flavors to meld together.
7. Serve: Enjoy this delightful salsa as a standalone salad or as a topping for grilled chicken, fish, or with a side of crispy tortilla chips.

Nutrition Information
(per serving):
- Calories: 220, Total Fat: 7g, Saturated Fat: 1g, Cholesterol: 0mg, Sodium: 210mg
- Total Carbohydrate: 34g, Dietary Fiber: 9g, Sugars: 11g, Protein: 8g
(Note: Nutritional values are approximate and may vary based on specific ingredients used.)

91. Butter Bean and Pickled Ginger Dip

This Butter Bean and Pickled Ginger Dip is a delightful fusion of creamy butter beans and tangy pickled ginger. It's a versatile dish that doubles as a dip or a spread, perfect for gatherings or a quick snack. Packed with protein and nutrients, it's a healthy addition to any meal or party spread.
Serving: Makes about 2 cups of dip, serving approximately 6 people.
Preparation time: 10 minutes
Ready time: 15 minutes

Ingredients:
- 2 cups cooked butter beans (or 1 can, drained and rinsed)
- 2 tablespoons pickled ginger, finely chopped
- 2 cloves garlic, minced
- 2 tablespoons tahini
- 2 tablespoons olive oil
- Juice of 1 lemon
- 1/4 teaspoon ground cumin
- Salt and pepper to taste
- Optional: chopped fresh parsley or cilantro for garnish

Instructions:
1. In a food processor, combine the butter beans, pickled ginger, minced garlic, tahini, olive oil, lemon juice, and ground cumin.
2. Blend the mixture until smooth and creamy. If needed, add a splash of water to achieve your desired consistency.
3. Taste and season with salt and pepper according to your preference. Adjust lemon juice or spices as desired.
4. Transfer the dip to a serving bowl. If you prefer, garnish with chopped fresh parsley or cilantro.
5. Serve the Butter Bean and Pickled Ginger Dip with your choice of fresh vegetables, pita bread, or crackers.

Nutrition Information
(per serving - about 1/3 cup):
- Calories: 150, Total Fat: 7g, Saturated Fat: 1g, Sodium: 200mg, Total Carbohydrates: 17g, Dietary Fiber: 5g, Sugars: 1g, Protein: 6g
(Note: Nutritional values are approximate and may vary based on specific ingredients used.)
This dip is a quick, nutritious option for any occasion. Enjoy its creamy texture and zesty flavors while benefiting from the healthy properties of butter beans!

92. Butter Bean and Chili Mango Salsa

This vibrant Butter Bean and Chili Mango Salsa is a testament to the versatility of butter beans. Blending the creaminess of butter beans with the sweetness of mango and a hint of spice from chili creates a salsa that's perfect as a topping or a side dish, bursting with flavors and nutrients.

Serving: Serves 4
Preparation Time: 15 minutes
Ready Time: 15 minutes

Ingredients:
- 1 can (15 oz) butter beans, drained and rinsed
- 1 ripe mango, diced
- 1 red bell pepper, diced
- 1 small red onion, finely chopped
- 1 jalapeño pepper, seeded and minced
- 1/4 cup fresh cilantro, chopped
- Juice of 2 limes
- 2 tablespoons olive oil
- Salt and pepper to taste

Instructions:
1. In a mixing bowl, combine the drained butter beans, diced mango, red bell pepper, red onion, jalapeño pepper, and chopped cilantro.
2. In a separate small bowl, whisk together the lime juice, olive oil, salt, and pepper.
3. Pour the dressing over the bean and mango mixture. Gently toss until all ingredients are well combined and coated with the dressing.
4. Adjust seasoning to taste.
5. Allow the salsa to sit for 5-10 minutes to let the flavors meld together before serving.

Nutrition Information
(per serving):
- Calories: 220, Total Fat: 7g, Saturated Fat: 1g, Cholesterol: 0mg, Sodium: 190mg
- Total Carbohydrate: 36g, Dietary Fiber: 9g, Sugars: 14g, Protein: 7g
This delightful salsa not only enhances the taste buds but also offers a healthy dose of fiber, vitamins, and plant-based protein, making it a fantastic addition to any meal or a standout appetizer at gatherings.

93. Butter Bean and Roasted Red Chili Hummus

Elevate your healthy eating game with this delightful Butter Bean and Roasted Red Chili Hummus recipe. Butter beans, also known as lima beans, bring a creamy texture to this classic Middle Eastern dip, while the addition of roasted red chili adds a subtle kick. Packed with protein, fiber, and essential nutrients, this hummus is not only delicious but also a nutritious choice for any occasion. Perfect as a dip, spread, or a wholesome snack, it's a versatile recipe that will become a staple in your healthy eating repertoire.

Serving: Makes approximately 2 cups of hummus.
Preparation Time: 15 minutes
Ready Time: 30 minutes

Ingredients:
- 2 cups cooked butter beans (canned or soaked and cooked)
- 1/4 cup tahini
- 3 tablespoons extra-virgin olive oil, plus extra for drizzling
- 1/4 cup fresh lemon juice
- 2 cloves garlic, minced
- 1 teaspoon ground cumin
- 1 teaspoon smoked paprika
- 1/2 teaspoon salt, or to taste
- 1/2 cup roasted red chili peppers, peeled and chopped
- Water (as needed for desired consistency)

Instructions:
1. If you haven't done so already, cook the butter beans by either using canned beans or soaking and boiling dried beans until tender. Drain and set aside.
2. In a food processor, combine the cooked butter beans, tahini, olive oil, lemon juice, minced garlic, cumin, smoked paprika, and salt.
3. Blend the ingredients until smooth, stopping to scrape down the sides of the processor bowl as needed.
4. Add the roasted red chili peppers to the mixture and pulse until they are evenly distributed throughout the hummus.
5. If the hummus is too thick, add water, one tablespoon at a time, until you reach your desired consistency.

6. Taste and adjust the seasoning, adding more salt or lemon juice if needed.
7. Transfer the hummus to a serving bowl, drizzle with olive oil, and garnish with additional smoked paprika or chopped herbs if desired.
8. Serve with pita bread, vegetable sticks, or as a spread on sandwiches. Enjoy!

Nutrition Information:
(Per 2-tablespoon serving)
- Calories: 90, Protein: 3g, Fat: 6g, Carbohydrates: 8g, Fiber: 2g, Sugar: 0g, Sodium: 120mg
Note: Nutrition Information is approximate and may vary based on specific ingredients and serving sizes.

94. Butter Bean and Smoky Paprika Pesto

Discover the delightful fusion of creamy butter beans and the rich, smoky flavor of paprika in this nutritious and flavorful Butter Bean and Smoky Paprika Pesto recipe. Packed with protein, fiber, and essential nutrients, this dish not only satisfies your taste buds but also nourishes your body. Perfect for those seeking healthy and hearty meal options, this recipe showcases the versatility of butter beans in a delicious and satisfying way.

Serving: 4 servings
Preparation Time: 15 minutes
Ready Time: 20 minutes

Ingredients:
- 2 cans (15 ounces each) butter beans, drained and rinsed
- 1/2 cup fresh basil leaves
- 1/3 cup grated Parmesan cheese
- 1/4 cup pine nuts, toasted
- 2 cloves garlic, minced
- 1 teaspoon smoked paprika
- 1/2 teaspoon salt
- 1/4 teaspoon black pepper
- 1/3 cup extra-virgin olive oil

- Juice of 1 lemon
- Zest of 1 lemon

Instructions:
1. In a food processor, combine the drained and rinsed butter beans, fresh basil leaves, Parmesan cheese, toasted pine nuts, minced garlic, smoked paprika, salt, and black pepper.
2. Pulse the ingredients until well combined and slightly chunky.
3. With the food processor running, slowly drizzle in the extra-virgin olive oil until the pesto reaches your desired consistency.
4. Add the lemon juice and lemon zest to the mixture, pulsing briefly to incorporate the citrusy flavors.
5. Taste and adjust the seasoning if necessary.
6. Transfer the Butter Bean and Smoky Paprika Pesto to a serving bowl.
7. Serve the pesto over whole-grain pasta, grilled chicken, or as a dip for fresh vegetables.

Nutrition Information:
Per Serving
- Calories: 320, Protein: 11g, Fat: 22g, Saturated Fat: 4g, Carbohydrates: 24g, Fiber: 6g, Sugar: 1g, Cholesterol: 8mg, Sodium: 490mg

Indulge in this wholesome and flavorful dish, showcasing the nutritional powerhouse of butter beans in a smoky and satisfying pesto. It's a delicious way to incorporate healthy ingredients into your everyday meals.

95. Butter Bean and Roasted Green Chile Salsa

Indulge your taste buds in a delightful journey with this Butter Bean and Roasted Green Chile Salsa – a vibrant and healthy addition to your culinary repertoire. Butter beans, rich in protein and fiber, blend seamlessly with the smoky allure of roasted green chilies, creating a salsa that's not only flavorful but also packed with nutritious goodness. This recipe perfectly encapsulates the essence of our cookbook, "Healthy Ways to Use Butter Beans Recipes," offering a versatile and delectable option for your dining table.

Serving: 4 servings

Preparation Time: 15 minutes
Ready Time: 30 minutes

Ingredients:
- 2 cups cooked butter beans, drained and rinsed
- 4 medium-sized green chilies, roasted and diced
- 1 cup cherry tomatoes, halved
- 1/2 red onion, finely chopped
- 2 cloves garlic, minced
- 1/4 cup fresh cilantro, chopped
- 2 tablespoons lime juice
- 2 tablespoons extra virgin olive oil
- Salt and pepper to taste

Instructions:
1. Roast the Green Chilies: Preheat the oven broiler. Place the green chilies on a baking sheet and roast under the broiler for 5-7 minutes, turning occasionally until the skin is charred. Remove from the oven, let them cool, and then dice them.
2. Prepare the Butter Beans: In a mixing bowl, combine the cooked butter beans, roasted green chilies, halved cherry tomatoes, chopped red onion, minced garlic, and fresh cilantro.
3. Whisk the Dressing: In a small bowl, whisk together lime juice, extra virgin olive oil, salt, and pepper to create a zesty dressing.
4. Combine and Toss: Pour the dressing over the bean mixture and gently toss until all ingredients are well coated.
5. Chill and Serve: Allow the salsa to chill in the refrigerator for at least 15 minutes to enhance the flavors. Serve chilled and enjoy as a refreshing side dish or a zingy topping for grilled meats.

Nutrition Information:
Per serving:
- Calories: 220, Protein: 8g, Carbohydrates: 30g, Dietary Fiber: 8g, Sugars: 4g, Fat: 9g, Saturated Fat: 1g, Cholesterol: 0mg, Sodium: 280mg
This Butter Bean and Roasted Green Chile Salsa is a wholesome and satisfying option for those seeking a nutritious and flavorful twist to traditional salsa recipes. Dive into a world of health and taste, and let the butter beans elevate your culinary experience.

96. Butter Bean and Cilantro Chimichurri

Elevate your culinary experience with this nutritious and flavorful Butter Bean and Cilantro Chimichurri recipe. Butter beans, known for their creamy texture and rich protein content, take center stage in this dish, creating a wholesome and satisfying meal. Paired with the vibrant freshness of cilantro chimichurri, this recipe not only tantalizes your taste buds but also provides a healthy dose of essential nutrients. Prepare to embark on a journey of deliciousness and nourishment with this delightful dish.

Serving: 4 servings
Preparation Time: 15 minutes
Ready Time: 25 minutes

Ingredients:
- 2 cans (15 ounces each) butter beans, drained and rinsed
- 1 cup fresh cilantro, finely chopped
- 3 cloves garlic, minced
- 1/4 cup red wine vinegar
- 1/2 cup extra-virgin olive oil
- 1 teaspoon red pepper flakes (adjust to taste)
- Salt and black pepper to taste

Instructions:
1. In a medium-sized mixing bowl, combine the drained and rinsed butter beans. Set aside.
2. In a separate bowl, prepare the cilantro chimichurri by mixing together the finely chopped cilantro, minced garlic, red wine vinegar, and red pepper flakes.
3. Gradually whisk in the extra-virgin olive oil into the cilantro mixture until well combined. Season with salt and black pepper to taste.
4. Pour the cilantro chimichurri over the butter beans and gently toss until the beans are evenly coated with the flavorful sauce.
5. Allow the dish to marinate for at least 10 minutes to let the flavors meld.
6. Serve the Butter Bean and Cilantro Chimichurri at room temperature or slightly chilled, allowing the beans to absorb the delicious chimichurri goodness.

Nutrition Information:

Note: Nutritional values are approximate and may vary based on specific ingredients used.
- Calories: 320 per serving, Protein: 12g, Carbohydrates: 22g, Dietary Fiber: 6g, Sugars: 1g, Fat: 22g, Saturated Fat: 3g, Cholesterol: 0mg, Sodium: 280mg

Indulge in this healthy and satisfying Butter Bean and Cilantro Chimichurri dish, perfect for those looking to incorporate butter beans into their diet in a deliciously innovative way.

97. Butter Bean and Cranberry Chutney

Elevate your culinary experience with this delightful Butter Bean and Cranberry Chutney—a perfect blend of creamy butter beans and the tart sweetness of cranberries. This recipe not only tantalizes your taste buds but also embodies the essence of healthy eating. Packed with essential nutrients, this chutney adds a burst of flavor to your meals while promoting a wholesome lifestyle. Discover the versatility of butter beans in this scrumptious creation that pairs well with various dishes.

Serving: Makes approximately 2 cups of chutney.
Preparation Time: 15 minutes
Ready Time: 45 minutes

Ingredients:
- 1 can (15 ounces) butter beans, drained and rinsed
- 1 cup fresh or frozen cranberries
- 1/2 cup red onion, finely chopped
- 1/4 cup apple cider vinegar
- 1/4 cup maple syrup or honey
- 1 teaspoon grated fresh ginger
- 1/2 teaspoon ground cinnamon
- 1/4 teaspoon ground cloves
- Salt and pepper to taste

Instructions:
1. In a medium saucepan, combine the drained butter beans, cranberries, chopped red onion, apple cider vinegar, and maple syrup (or honey).

2. Place the saucepan over medium heat and bring the mixture to a gentle boil. Reduce the heat to low and simmer for 25-30 minutes, or until the cranberries burst and the chutney thickens.

3. Stir in the grated fresh ginger, ground cinnamon, ground cloves, salt, and pepper. Continue to simmer for an additional 10-15 minutes, allowing the flavors to meld.

4. Taste the chutney and adjust the seasoning if necessary. If you prefer a sweeter chutney, you can add more maple syrup or honey.

5. Remove the saucepan from the heat and let the chutney cool to room temperature before transferring it to a storage container.

6. Refrigerate the chutney for at least 4 hours or overnight to allow the flavors to fully develop.

7. Serve chilled or at room temperature. This Butter Bean and Cranberry Chutney pairs wonderfully with grilled chicken, roasted vegetables, or as a topping for whole grain crackers.

Nutrition Information:
(Per 2-tablespoon serving)
- Calories: 40, Total Fat: 0.2g, Cholesterol: 0mg, Sodium: 45mg, Total Carbohydrates: 9g, Dietary Fiber: 1.5g, Sugars: 4g, Protein: 1g

Indulge in the wholesome goodness of this Butter Bean and Cranberry Chutney, a nutritious addition to your culinary repertoire.

98. Butter Bean and Walnut-Basil Pesto

Elevate your culinary experience with this nutritious and flavorful Butter Bean and Walnut-Basil Pesto. Butter beans, also known as lima beans, bring a creamy texture to this pesto, complemented by the rich and earthy notes of walnuts. This dish is not only a feast for the taste buds but also a celebration of wholesome, plant-based ingredients. Whether served as a dip, spread, or pasta sauce, this recipe is a versatile and delightful addition to your healthy eating repertoire.

Serving: 4 servings
Preparation Time: 15 minutes
Ready Time: 20 minutes

Ingredients:

- 2 cups cooked butter beans (canned or boiled)
- 1/2 cup walnuts, toasted
- 2 cups fresh basil leaves, packed
- 3 cloves garlic, minced
- 1/2 cup nutritional yeast
- 1/2 cup extra-virgin olive oil
- Juice of 1 lemon
- Salt and pepper to taste

Instructions:
1. Prepare the Butter Beans:
- If using canned butter beans, drain and rinse them thoroughly. If using dried beans, cook according to package instructions until tender.
2. Toast the Walnuts:
- In a dry skillet over medium heat, toast the walnuts until they become fragrant and slightly golden. Be attentive to prevent burning. Set aside to cool.
3. Blend

Ingredients:
- In a food processor, combine the cooked butter beans, toasted walnuts, basil leaves, minced garlic, nutritional yeast, and lemon juice. Pulse until the mixture begins to combine.
4. Add Olive Oil:
- With the food processor running, slowly pour in the extra-virgin olive oil. Continue blending until the pesto reaches a smooth and creamy consistency.
5. Season to Taste:
- Taste the pesto and season with salt and pepper as needed. Adjust the lemon juice or nutritional yeast to achieve the desired flavor.
6. Serve:
- Spoon the Butter Bean and Walnut-Basil Pesto into a bowl. Drizzle with a bit of extra olive oil and garnish with fresh basil leaves. Serve as a dip with vegetables, spread on crackers, or toss with your favorite pasta.

Nutrition Information:
(Per Serving)
- Calories: 350, Total Fat: 28g, Saturated Fat: 4g, Trans Fat: 0g, Cholesterol: 0mg, Sodium: 150mg, Total Carbohydrates: 18g, Dietary Fiber: 6g, Sugars: 1g, Protein: 10g

Indulge in the wholesome goodness of this Butter Bean and Walnut-Basil Pesto – a nutritious and delicious twist on traditional pesto that will leave you satisfied and nourished.

99. Butter Bean and Charred Lemon Hummus

This delightful Butter Bean and Charred Lemon Hummus is a testament to the versatility of butter beans. Creamy, tangy, and infused with the smoky essence of charred lemons, this hummus makes for a flavorful, nutritious spread or dip. Rich in protein and fiber, it's a healthy addition to any meal or snack.

Serving:
- Serves: 6-8

Preparation time:
- Prep: 15 minutes

Ready time:
- Ready in: 20 minutes

Ingredients:
- 2 cans (15 oz each) butter beans, drained and rinsed
- 2 lemons
- 3 tablespoons tahini
- 2 garlic cloves, minced
- 2 tablespoons olive oil
- 1/2 teaspoon ground cumin
- Salt and pepper to taste
- 2 tablespoons water (or more for desired consistency)
- Paprika and fresh parsley for garnish (optional)

Instructions:
1. Char the Lemons:
- Cut the lemons in half and place them cut-side down on a preheated grill or skillet over medium-high heat.
- Cook until the lemons develop charred marks, about 4-5 minutes. Remove and set aside to cool.

2. Prepare the Hummus:
- In a food processor, combine the drained butter beans, tahini, minced garlic, olive oil, cumin, salt, and pepper.

- Squeeze the juice from the charred lemons into the processor. Be cautious of seeds; a strainer can be used to catch them.
- Blend the ingredients until smooth, scraping down the sides as needed.

3. Adjust Consistency:
- While blending, add water gradually until the hummus reaches your desired consistency. Add more for a smoother texture.

4. Serve:
- Transfer the hummus to a serving bowl. Drizzle with a touch of olive oil and sprinkle paprika and fresh parsley for garnish if desired.

Nutrition Information
(per serving):
- Calories: 180, Total Fat: 8g, Saturated Fat: 1g, Trans Fat: 0g, Cholesterol: 0mg, Sodium: 220mg
- Total Carbohydrate: 21g, Dietary Fiber: 6g
- Total Sugars: 1g
- Added Sugars: 0g, Protein: 7g

Nutritional values are approximate and may vary based on specific ingredients used. Adjustments can be made to suit dietary preferences or restrictions. Enjoy this vibrant and healthy hummus as a dip for veggies, spread on sandwiches, or as a flavorful accompaniment to meals!

100. Butter Bean and Za'atar Pesto

Butter beans, with their creamy texture and mild flavor, are a versatile addition to any kitchen. When paired with the vibrant and aromatic Za'atar pesto, they create a dish that's not only delicious but also packed with nutrients. This recipe combines the earthy goodness of butter beans with the zesty, herby flavors of Za'atar, resulting in a delightful and healthy meal or side dish.

Serving: 4 servings
Preparation time: 15 minutes
Ready time: 20 minutes

Ingredients:
- 2 cups cooked butter beans
- 1/4 cup fresh parsley, chopped

- 1/4 cup fresh basil leaves
- 2 tablespoons Za'atar spice blend
- 2 cloves garlic, minced
- 1/4 cup walnuts or pine nuts
- 1/4 cup grated Parmesan cheese (optional for a non-vegan version)
- 1/4 cup olive oil
- Juice of 1/2 lemon
- Salt and pepper to taste

Instructions:
1. Prepare Butter Beans: If you're using canned butter beans, drain and rinse them thoroughly. If using dried beans, cook them according to package instructions until they're tender.
2. Make Za'atar Pesto: In a food processor, combine the parsley, basil, Za'atar spice blend, minced garlic, nuts, and Parmesan cheese (if using). Pulse until the ingredients are roughly chopped.
3. Add Olive Oil and Lemon Juice: While the food processor is running, slowly pour in the olive oil and lemon juice. Continue blending until the mixture reaches a smooth, pesto-like consistency. Add salt and pepper to taste and blend again briefly to incorporate.
4. Combine with Butter Beans: In a mixing bowl, toss the cooked butter beans with the prepared Za'atar pesto until the beans are evenly coated.
5. Serve: Transfer the butter bean and Za'atar pesto mixture to a serving dish. You can garnish it with additional chopped parsley or a sprinkle of Za'atar spice blend for an extra burst of flavor.

Nutrition Information
(approximate values per serving):
- Calories: 280, Total Fat: 18g, Saturated Fat: 2.5g, Cholesterol: 0mg, Sodium: 180mg, Total Carbohydrates: 23g, Dietary Fiber: 6g, Sugars: 1g, Protein: 9g

Enjoy this dish warm or cold, as a protein-rich main or a hearty side, and savor the fusion of Mediterranean flavors with the wholesome goodness of butter beans!

CONCLUSION

Butter Bean Bliss: 100 Healthy Ways to Savor this Versatile Legume" celebrates the humble butter bean in its myriad forms and culinary possibilities. Throughout this cookbook, we have explored diverse recipes that showcase the butter bean's versatility, from hearty soups and stews to vibrant salads and innovative dips. By delving into its nutritional benefits and culinary adaptability, this collection aims to inspire and educate readers on integrating this nutritious legume into their daily meals.

At the heart of "Butter Bean Bliss" lies a commitment to promoting health and wellness through accessible, flavorful dishes. Butter beans, with their creamy texture and mild flavor, provide a perfect canvas for both traditional and innovative cooking techniques. Whether blended into creamy hummus, tossed into a robust chili, or mixed into a refreshing summer salad, butter beans offer endless opportunities to enhance dishes with their protein-rich goodness.

Moreover, this cookbook emphasizes the importance of sustainability and mindful eating. Butter beans, as a sustainable protein source, contribute to a balanced diet while supporting environmentally conscious food choices. By incorporating more plant-based meals into our culinary repertoire, we not only nourish our bodies but also contribute positively to the planet.

Throughout these pages, we have also explored the cultural significance of butter beans in various cuisines around the world. From Mediterranean-inspired dishes to Southern comfort classics, each recipe tells a story of heritage and culinary evolution. By embracing these diverse influences, "Butter Bean Bliss" encourages a deeper appreciation for global flavors and traditions.

In conclusion, "Butter Bean Bliss: 100 Healthy Ways to Savor this Versatile Legume" is more than just a collection of recipes; it is a culinary journey that celebrates the richness of butter beans and their potential to transform everyday meals into nourishing experiences. Whether you are a seasoned cook or a novice in the kitchen, this cookbook invites you to explore, experiment, and enjoy the simple pleasures of cooking with butter beans. Let this cookbook be your guide to discovering the joy of wholesome, delicious meals that prioritize both flavor and nutrition. Here's to savoring the blissful versatility of butter beans, one delightful dish at a time.